All
Souls

All Souls

Essential Poems

Brenda Marie Osbey

Louisiana
State
University
Press
Baton Rouge

Published by Louisiana State University Press
Copyright © 2015 by Brenda Marie Osbey
All rights reserved
Manufactured in the United States of America
LSU Press Paperback Original
First printing

DESIGNER: *Mandy McDonald Scallan*
TYPEFACE: *Calluna*

Library of Congress Cataloging-in-Publication Data

Osbey, Brenda Marie.
 [Poems. Selections]
 All souls : essential poems / Brenda Marie Osbey
pages ; cm
 ISBN 978-0-8071-6200-2 (cloth : alk. paper) — ISBN
978-0-8071-6201-9 (pdf) — ISBN 978-0-8071-6202-6
(epub) — ISBN 978-0-8071-6203-3 (mobi)
 I. Title.
 PS3565.S33A6 2015
 811'54—dc23

                                        2015011996

Lois Emelda Hamilton
1930–2010

who sings

breath
bone
song
prayer
blood
marrow
Mother

In Memoriam

Contents

Acknowledgments . xi

Prologue: *Widows of Tremé* . xiii

1. HOUSE IN THE FAUBOURG

The House in the Street Where Memory Lives . 3

Faubourg . 5

The Old Women on Burgundy Street . 7

Living in the Tan House . 9

Madhouses . 15

Ramona Véagis . 20

Chifalta . 26

Ceremony for Minneconjoux . 31

Elvena . 42

Faubourg Study: Rain . 47

Regina . 55

Memory No. 2 . 57

Faubourg Study: Blood . 61

Morning . 68

Faubourg Study No. 3: *The Seven Sisters of New Orleans* . 70

House of Mercies . 90

The House . 91

2. MOURNING LIKE A SKIN

Peculiar Fascination with the Dead . 99

Stones of Soweto . 111

Another Time and Farther South . 116
Requiem for a Chief . 118
For Charles H. Rowell, on the Death of His Father . 121
Requiem for a Tall Man . 124
Alberta (*Factory Poem / Variation 2*) . 128

3. SOMETHING ABOUT TRAINS

Speaking of Trains . 137
New Train Study . 146

4. LITTLE HISTORY, PART ONE

Qu'on Arrive Enfin . 155
Slaves to the City . 159
The Business of Pursuit: San Malo's Prayer . 161
The Head of Luís Congo Speaks . 168
DOM-TOM Primer . 174
Regarding the Intermediate Travels of Cristóval Colón . 179
History . 190
Canne à Sucre: A Slave-Song Suite . 210

5. UNFINISHED COFFEES

Everything Happens to (Monk and) Me . 219
Expeditus . 224
The Evening News: A Letter to Nina Simone . 229
Litany of Our Lady . 238
Suicide City . 240

6. WHAT HUNGER

Desire and Private Griefs . 251

House of the Dead Remembering (*House of Mercies / Variation 2*) . 257

Evidence of Conjure . 261

Freeing Your Hands . 266

Movement 1 / part one . 268

Against the Bone . 271

Memory No. 1 . 272

The Wastrel-Woman Poem . 276

Glossary and Notes . 279

Author Biography . 295

Acknowledgments

Poems included here were published in previous volumes of mine, and I gratefully acknowledge *Callaloo* and the Callaloo Poetry Series; Wesleyan University Press; Story Line Press; *The Southern Review* and Louisiana State University Press; and Time Being Books.

Some poems were published also, sometimes in-progress or as excerpts, in journals and periodicals. Grateful acknowledgment is made also to the publishers and editors of *Atlantic Studies: Literary, Historical and Cultural Perspectives; Renaissance Noire; American Voice; Southern Exposure; Greenfield Review; 2PLUS2: A Collection of International Writing; Illuminations: An International Magazine of Contemporary Writing; Southern Literary Journal; Mondes Francophones; American Poetry Review; Poet Lore;* and *War|Scapes.*

Prologue

the widows open wide their doors each morning
dash fresh water on their steps
to move any evil
blocking their paths that day
to show
that they themselves are clean
pure
that they have nothing within to hide
no evil of their own to work
and no new man

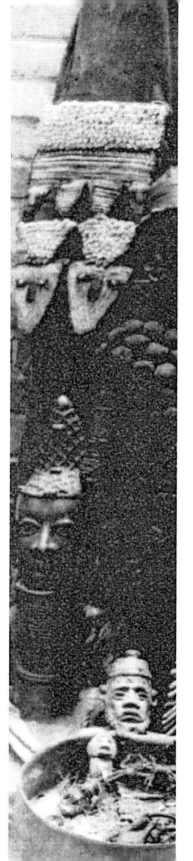

I.

house in the faubourg

The House in the Street Where Memory Lives

i sit at the front parlor window
i touch memory with the tips of my fingers
the back of my tongue—
it falls apart—
the old woman
the man who is old now and alone up at manchac
alone in all that swamp—
it falls apart:
memory
the years and all their days
rolling a little from place to place
the visions that dry before they can be grasped
visions that dance in the hard sunlight
stretched long across the floor.

bamba
sweet basil
the stocking-feet of my mother's friend
the good hands of a man
death and betrayal
the turning away
small senseless words like *please*—
what good is any of this to me now?
to anyone?
it falls apart.
it falls.

here is my chest all bone and fleshless skin
with almost no breast to cling to
my hips below
my belly
hands of a woman
hands of a man
it is falling.
it is falling now.
far into the night it falls—
bamba sweet basil
the thrashing of bones
the witch of sleep
the caul come down.
and there is the city, the street
here, the house my mother built
the house my mother built around us
asks the same questions my mother asked.

i do not answer.
this is my house.

Faubourg

the faubourg is a city within the larger city
and the women walk in pairs and clusters
moving along the slave-bricked streets
wearing print dresses
carrying parcels
on their hips or heads.

within the small city of the faubourg
there is always work to be done:
rooms and yards and laundry to see to
and always some trouble
to be put to rest.
burdens to be shifted
from an arm to a hip
from a hip to the head.
there are children to be scolded and sung to.
there are wares to call out
to sell or buy or search for at market.
and along the narrow banqettes leading there—
a cook
a seamstress
a day's-work-woman to find or be found.
there are chickens to feel and buy
and get their necks wrung.
palm oil to buy and sell
palm wine
hot sweet potato pies.
and there are blues to be sung or heard
above the trees and rooftops
all hours of the day and night.

the dead must be mourned and sung over
and prayers told them to carry to the other side.
the dead must be chanted and marched to their tombs
and the tombs then tended and the dogs kept away.
yatta leaves must be dried and woven into belts and baskets.
rags must be burned in sulphur to ward off mosquitoes
and slave brick crushed and scrubbed across doorways.
there is love to be made
conju to be worked.

and quiet as it is kept
most anything can be done in the faubourg.

in such a city
what name is good for a woman?
in such a city
what good is any woman's name?

The Old Women on Burgundy Street

the old women on burgundy street
braid the years
into their grey-brown-white hair.
they put patient time
into the pinning of a plait
braiding in equal
ones and twos.

for various reasons
some will braid by morning
or late evening
after supper songs
after dishes and cats
have been put away.
only once or twice
have i seen one braiding at noon.

the old women on burgundy street
drink bourbon from coffee cups
while the sun goes down.
it cures rheumatism
gout
and ailments left over
from the change-of-life.

they braid in french braids
a neat basket weave
that does not interfere
with a profile
or a bowed-down head.

some of them i have seen
braiding songs into their hair
sipping from those coffee cups
sitting out on front porches
or just inside
an open sidelight.
they do not moan.
their songs have an air
of learned resignation.

Living in the Tan House

I.

what did percy jerome mean
marrying me
and locking me up in that big block of wood
on calliope street i never will know
but he's dead
and i can't say it matters now
i got my godchild marie steel
to come up here and live
watch me and the house just in case
she's about as good as they come
just stays in church is all

2.

he came from off tennessee street
that was before i knew him
in the back of my mind
i guess i must have wanted him even then
but there is talk
and so you keep silent about such things
until someone else
brings them to your notice
so i suppose i wanted him
those years he was living round aunt gert
before i ever knew of him
or at least
that's what he said
once he'd come to court me

somehow i never understood
that it meant we would marry
everyone said that was foolishness
and what did i know—
a girl of nineteen
knowing what a grown man of thirty-seven should do?
we married then
and two years later
he bought this unsightly house
and had it painted tan
people coming into the neighborhood looking for me
the old folk would say
"lavinia, miss theophile's daughter?
she's living in that tan house up the street"
finally that was how everybody called it
"that tan house"
and so did i
after time had passed

3.

things went alright
percy jerome treated me good
took care of the note
but i needed something
i really did just need something
i tried to tell percy jerome
but all he could figure
was having a baby
like having a baby was supposed to do something for me
and when he commenced to talking like so
i set him straight
and learnt all over again
to make do without words
but i still needed something
and when i would go out late of a night
and work my garden
it was like i could feel this something
pulling me
just pulling at me from down under the ground
and that was how i discovered my throat
and commenced to singing
people'd say
"lavinia, ms. theophile's daughter,
we never knew she could sing before"
they never did
because i never did
till one night my throat opened up
and i commenced to singing
it was like hearing a language that never had been
it was like having a whole other woman
standing in your middle
and singing out your insides
and to tell the truth as i know it
i still cannot find the words

4.
my voice is an okono drum
for sacred rituals
this whole city i move in
moves to the left
two steps at a time
to the songs i declare

5.

mr. p. c. ubain moved next door to us
five years later
he was an old gentleman from pointe-à-la-hâche
collected bits of thread from people
was making this tapestry thing
which he called history
old p. c. ubain didn't bother a soul
except to get his cuts of string
he would step out his backdoor
to hear me singing at night
he said nothing at all
i could see him through the hidden-lily
and i knew he was listening
mr. p. c. ubain was listening at me

6.
this song has no words
i am singing this song
from a place i have not known
i am singing without words
i need to say those things
for which no words are coined
my soul is a rice field
and this voice
ancient hum
first waters
original soliloquy
for my soul is laid down.

Madhouses

I.
these women men business
burn their hair only on the ends
and spit tobacco
in the reverend's hedges
they call themselves
mothers
and wear bare feet in public
daring fathers and brothers
to come down on the banqette
and i have seen them dancing
along the interstate in mid-january

we call them madhouses
but it is only that we fear
i know their secrets
only through having learned them
the hardest way

my name is felicity
i live inside the city
i am telling only
as much as you can bear

2.
the bahalia women are coming
from round st. james
carrying the bamba-root
in their hands
believe on those hands
and they will see you through seasons
of drought and flood
believe on these hands
and you will cross the grandy-water

3.
journey with me and see what i see

first you hear the leaves
past silence
hitting the ground
moving along the streets
with an undercurrent of rhythm
moving to your bloodbeat
and the sounds of your hands
reaching
reaching up

4.
just before you see them
there is their confounded
jingling
the sound of those root ends
against their tambourines
but no one really hears them coming
just the thud of those bare feet
against the broken surfaces
of the banqette
the low rumbling of song
and then bahalia
bahalia
and yet
you can never say you heard them

it is like that
their coming

5.
it is not tonight i will find the path
i am ready, damballah
but the way is barred

a slender woman in red skirts
tignon and golden hoops through her ears
young and smooth
and jerking to the sound
of old blood
and thin-skinned men
walking on the graves of the old ones

i am ready, oh spirit
but the way is dark

6.
and like rising from a dream
they are gone
and like a vision they never leave you

standing in my sidelight
you can see them
women so far gone
that their walking is dance
madhouses so grey
against the other houses and churches
that you pretend for now
you do not see them
and never did

but when you make the final journey
and stand at the crossing
seeking the barred footing
it was i who first showed you
and remember my name
it was felicity who told you
how to exit one madhouse
and enter the other

Ramona Véagis

in 1916 ramona véagis fell off the side of the world
she filled the bathtub to overflowing
and sat down in a kitchen chair
in the middle of the water.
when miss lucille and mister eddy did knock through that door
there was water everywhere
and the children had to be sent outdoors.

they always said she went off that way
on account of them not letting her marry lejean
except i remember when ramona véagis come to me
and told me
said she had fallen off the world
and could not climb back on

2.

it is done this way
i am quite sure this is how it's done
you run around and around
the circumference of your world so fast
that you can not possibly fall off
still there is some secret i seem to have forgot.
help me ms. regina
i know you ought to know
help me stay on my world
or else there is no one i can go to

3.

ramona véagis come up these front steps
like it was a thing she done all her life
and when she looked up at me
out of all that écru
and that feather hat
i could see in her forehead
all the lights and shapes that child had broken into
like jewels of shattered crystal
on the sitting room parquet

4.
in the morning-before-day
i used to wake up in a clutter of voices
i should have known
i should never have trusted them
or maybe i told lejean
he was still coming for me in the evenings then
so maybe i told him
and maybe that was why
but saturday before last everything shifted
mamma lucille hit me across the back with a dustmop handle
and that was the first thing
that was how i took to my bed
it was nothing lejean and his people put on me
it truly wasn't
mamma struck me with that mop handle
and i took to my bed
and when i woke up that evening
and she was sitting there looking so worried
that was the third thing
when i bit her in the face and saw the purple blood run down
that was when
because before then
i truly was quite safe
i never thought i'd come here ms. regina
i never thought because look
how did i know i should commence
to falling off the world
all of a sudden
now?

5.

ramona véagis come here
looking for me to give her roots
looking for me to moan and step over her
for me to heal her
and knowing i could not
i'm sure she knew
even when she first came
her eyes
coming out of all that écru
said i was not to blame
said all i could do
was to sit with her into evening
watching her hands
rise and fall
with my white lace curtains
blowing up over our heads
on the little settee

6.

ms. regina can not help me
she can not break my fall
i am moving way too fast
to be caught up in even a chamy bag
i speak these words
in one of many voices
and already
even now
the world from which you hear me
is so many fallings from my sphere
i have fallen so fast
you will think perhaps
you do you not hear me calling
at all

Chifalta

I.
kiss me
here
she said
right here
in the center
of my hand
why do you hesitate?
those are only
blues
what are you
afraid of?
that you might not
die
if you
struggle somewhat?

2.
there was a catalpa tree
quite alone
among the other trees
the heavy
mottled
flowers
fall easily
with the slightest breeze
and do you think
i have spent all this time
sheltering myself
building this outer hull
only to be drawn in
like the rest of them?

3.
they are lonely
they are lonely
they bend over in semi-circles
groveling after their own insides
unable to touch
even themselves
someone should show them how easy it is
to touch their own bellies
head to center
arms encircling
in easy
spherical
motions
i have done so
i have done so

4.
mother
mother
the catalpa tree will die
it is folding itself
and afraid to bear flowers
mother
mother
the catalpa tree is bending
it is folding itself
and afraid to bear flowers

why are you calling me
why are you calling me
i was shucking oysters last evening and i heard you
singing
what do want of me?
all i have
is sayings
and pearls

5.
in a dream just now broken
beneath the catalpa tree
i kissed her palms
and rolled into a song
of weary
purging
nightcalls
when i awaken
she is laughing
i have done so
i have done so
mother   mother
i have done so

6.
i am no longer sure
what struggling is

7.
go away from me
chifalta
i can not bear your madness
and my own as well.

Ceremony for Minneconjoux

it was years back you know
down bayou la fouche
she named her daughter
minneconjoux
so that people would not mistake
her indian blood

it was just a lean-to
right up against the water's edge
she said herself
that he would take her out in the damp
never inside
that's what she called it
taking her
she said when they did it out there
his two black greasy plaits
brushing her shoulders
his chest up
away from her
so he could smile down on her
it was not so far
from the slavery her grandmother
had raised her on
a creole woman
fanning herself
recording with her eyes
what happened to the other women
on le compte's land

it was 1943
he came
mostly just passing
in and out the neighborhood
looking just like a mardi gras indian
from off dumaine street
that's what everyone said he was
until mamma lou
called him up the front walk
and asked him what he was
and where he belonged to
he was a choctaw man
but mamma lou says
she knew choctaws to be squat
and ducky
she told him about
l'il ms. lincoln
with the choctaw blood in her
he repeated it
he was a choctaw man
this time adding
full-blooded
and picking at his teeth
with a sliver
of van-van she had growing
out there.
next day
he was up on the porch
conversing with mamma lou
about hard-to-find-work
and low-down-white-folks.

soon after the season broke
he come to work for mamma lou
that's when lenazette saw him
for the first time
he wasn't much lighter than her
with two plaits
and a woven head-band.
she come through the run-down page-fence gate
and looked up at him on the ladder
what the hell was he doing?
she meant to know
he smiled
mamma lou had hired him to fix up.
her face got real evil when she asked him
who?
ms. philemon he said this time
lenazette went up them stairs
and slammed the door
hard.

lenazette had just finished
from old madame markham's school
that winter he was
walking the streets
looking like a mardi gras
she was sixteen
and wore her hair in french braids
in two buns
on the sides of her head
that spring
he was fixing the windows one day
it was warm
lenazette was at the dresser
about to turn up her hair
when he called in for water
she brought it
not bothering to cover up
the white cotton slip she wore
when she leaned out
she said he could have tea
it had been on ice since last evening
he said
just water
he stood on that ladder
staring down at her slip straps
and again at her braids
i want to touch them
sometime
was what he said
she looked at him
your hands are dirty
he drank the water straight down
they can be cleaned
without much difficulty
he said.

mamma lou paid him every week
and fed him once a day
i was to bring him water
when he asked
it began to be sticky
around the house
i wore a white cotton slip
and an eyelet bed jacket
i wore my braids down now
connected together at the ends
i have always liked things
connected together at the ends
after a while
we could talk
he knew french
i still spoke patois
despite ms. markham's switchings
he understood me
but could only answer in french
that was the first thing
i learned from him.

one day
out on the back porch
i had these culottes on
and a white blouse
he'd come around for water
more than water
he said that mamma had told him
about her mamma
and le compte's place
we talked about that
about how me and mamma
come to look like we did
and how i could go to markham's
but mostly we talked about slaves
and stolen land
he said the food was real good
i told him mamma did the cooking
he said to let him comb my hair
i said it was already combed
he undid it without my say-so
i don't know how much mamma heard
but when i looked up
she was watching him combing in my hair
when she called me in
i told her he didn't mean no harm
she looked out past me
i ain't told you a damn thing about harm
girl
not a goddamn thing
days later
when i walked up on them talking
they hushed up

in june
i went with him to bayou la fouche
i sat sewing
while he built the house around me
when i asked how come we just had one room
he told me what-all we had to
we could do there
i was sewing dresses
there was ceremony
holding hands
down on our knees at the water
for weeks i waited
he never touched me
until that one-room was finished
after i lost the first child
he never touched me for six months
not like that anyhow

every night he'd take down my hair
and comb in it

that's when we started going outside
and that's how you come
when i let him
start to combing in my hair again.

he would look down on me
two oily plaits
slapping my neck
and shoulders
i would try not to look

mostly he worked the riverfront
bringing home crates of fruit
vegetables
he never would eat rice
till he saw me feeding it to you

in the evenings
or sometimes early in the morning-before-day
he would pull me by the hand
and lead me out to the sycamore tree
he'd just hold on to me
with his arms up on my shoulders
then we'd be down in the grass
and i could see his eyes
i used to tell him you might see
he said one day you would
when i reached up
i knew he was forcing me
making me need what i didn't want
and i started waiting for him to come
and start to combing in my hair
i would hear him mumbling
but i didn't want to know
didn't want to understand
what he was saying
i told him to stop it
and he wouldn't
i tried to move from under him
but his legs pinned me down
he was smiling
and mumbling
and making sounds
and when i saw you in the door
i told him to stop
and he wouldn't
and i picked up a stone
and beat him in his head

when i was ten
i left mamma zette
to go live in the city
with mamma lou
she had fine smooth hands
and she oiled my hair
when i was twelve
she cut it off
i asked her if it was because
that peterson boy climbed the fence
to talk to me
and put his hands in my hair
i asked her if it was because
my papa sat up ontop my mamma
holding on her braids
that's when she slapped me
i remember her face when she slapped me
when she died
she told me mamma
had been in charity
then jackson
i looked for papa
up at the bayou
la fouche was empty
the lean-to was not even locked
i found a woman there
her body nothing more
than a cedar switch
i have her picture now
on my bureau
she spoke low
sitting on the floor
sewing dresses
talking of child-having
and other ceremonies

i am minneconjoux.
i live in the house on st. claude street.
i connect myself
to the used thing
i keep on my bureau.
at mardi gras time
i stand on the walk-way
and watch the indians
dancing off dumaine.

Elvena

I.
there is a house down on old roman street
all the women pass through.
one stands outside the gate
bare feet
broad skirts gathered loose
about her hips.
have you lost anything today?
tell me, neighbor
what have you lost today?
and her madness is a conju
slung like rope about the heart.
i said i feel her madness like a conju
like a rope
slung round my heart.

do you see elvena?
she got that way touching neighbor-women
on the edges of their fingers.
do you see that bone-step walk she walks?
and the women who go by
looking past her face
past the ash-black hands
pretending they do not see her
and nothing has been lost?
a woman can go so far out
there never will be a way back.
and there are things a woman will do
can't be learned
and won't be understood.
but somebody's got to be a witness.
don't tell me you don't see that woman
moving barefoot along the banqette.

2.

a woman goes barefoot along the banqette this evening.
no one speaks her name.
the neighbor-people have difficulty recalling her—
and no one ever remembers a woman
as she once was

there is a neighbor-woman out there
a long ways from shoring
throw out your shimmy straps
and roll that woman in

who will touch her now?
who?
the mothers with their prayer-bands
wound tight about their wrists and waists?
the widows stabbing bricked pavements
with their low-heeled shoes,
little beads of sweat just visible above the lips,
the pearls of mourning strung effortless across their bosoms?
maybe the younger sisters she taught so well,
the school-girls who skip and prance with ease?
or else the ones riding by
on hips a man would shout over?
a neighbor-woman stands outside the gate this evening.
somebody's got to be a witness
somebody ought to call her name

3.
i used to be a woman other people called by name.
lived in a house
where the blues clung to the ceilings
to all the doors and the side-porch
and all around my garden
out back of the house.
i used to go to that garden
and sing all the blues i could find.
you'd be surprised how much blues can grow
between the hidden-lily and the monkey-grass
overnight.

the man next door
was from somewhere out in the country.
was making a kind of cloth.
worked at it all the time.
i would see him standing back in the shadows.
i could tell he was listening
and sometimes i thought he said my name—
as if it meant something.
he never did.
just stood there in the shadows
working that cloth
and listening to my blues.
sometimes i wondered
what kind of blues
that man had learned to make or give.
and sometimes i wondered
if he put my song into that cloth.
and what he might have lost besides.

and tell me, neighbor
what have you lost today?

4.
only the bone-step women
would ever come for her in broad daylight
carrying their satchels of longing
like easy parcels on turbaned heads.
carrying that woman along
between the folds of their red cotton skirts
calling aloud, to no one in particular
tell the truth
tell the truth and do right
carrying that woman along like one more burden
one more parcel
that amounts to nothing much
moving along the broken road
that leads to bayou st. john.

elvena could walk among them
bare feet keeping time
to the bones up on their heads.
tell the truth, i could hear them shout.
tell the truth and do right
i know you are a witness
just tell the truth and do right

5.
the bone-step women do not come.
i sit on my front-porch into the night.
i am working colored cloth
from cuts of used string.
i see elvena when she steps down from the banqette.
i see her step
into the empty street
ash-black hands turned out
palms facing toward me.
i hold up the unfinished cloth-piece
and she begins to sing:

tell me, neighbor
what that blues is made from
tell me
tell me
i want to know
what have you lost today?

Faubourg Study: Rain

("the devil is beating his wife")

the devil is beating his wife again.
almost everyone knows he means to kill her this time.
no one moves a muscle.

every day between one and four o'clock it rains.
and on the days when it does not rain between one and four
it storms like hell from midnight on.

the earth is thoroughly soaked.
everything is in bloom—
brick and stone and wooden walls and fences gates and doors
spawn their greenish grayish yellowish moss.

there are more full-term pregnancies this summer than usual
fewer stabbings and shootings.
or so they say.

imagine also
that it is thoroughly righteously
hot—
what here is politely called *sultry.*
we are at the outset still
of what is likely to be
a busy and a fruitful
hurricane season.

this is of course
the city of my birth.
i have seen such summers before.

2.

she was barefoot.
that was the first thing, i recall.
here it was february—
kind of toward the end of february—
and there'd been a hard freeze a few nights before.
and here she was
standing at the head of the market
barefoot as a corpse.
so i go up to her
and she kind of tilts her head like maybe
she could be hard of hearing, you know.
and before i can say word the first
she heads out toward the esplanade.
just starts on off
like that,
here she snaps her fingers.
you know?
i mean
i wouldn't say she was running—
let's just say she wasn't wasting time.

3.
prelude:
when you get to the crossroads
there is a tendency always just to stand a while.
you go ahead then.
only
get down low—squat like—
behind pressed right up against your heels.
go on and
get low.
stay there like that a while—
long as you care to.
long as you can.
you will want
to remember this
before it's done with.

4.
when you—1, 2, 3, 4—
get to the cross in the road
have mercy—when you—3, 4—
get to the cross in the road
i say you
when you

5.

well.
i had just taken down the wash
because amelie next door
had yelled out cross the back fence that the rain was about to start.
and sure enough
just as i'd rolled those last few pieces into the basket
here come the first giant drops.
hard too.

she licks her front teeth as if to
set them straight.
they are pearlescent
giving the impression of a certain
fragility—
until she bites
into the bone of the fish she has just finished stripping all but bare.

well.
amelie and me passed some
one or two words as i was heading back up the steps.
and i almost fell down dead on the spot
*cause there **she** was*
sitting just as prim as you please
about midway up the back steps—
my back steps.
so when amelie hollers
"see you got yourself some company today too"
i figure it's alright.
you know i mean
like at least i'm not crazy or nothing.
at least she's really real and all.
well anyhow
we'll get back to that part later.

"looks like you need to get yourself in out this rain, little sister," i tells her.
and if that child opened her mouth
then moses left his tablets on the mount and come down and baked me a cake.
she just picks herself up
hands behind her back, you know, hiding something,
and follows me on inside.
"what you got there little sister" i asks her
trying to get her to warm to me some, you know.
"what you got there?"
and she pulls her hands out real slow like in a magic show.
so i tap the right one.
nothing.
then i tap the left one
and she turns that one over real slow too, only she keeps it closed up tight-tight.
so now i'm getting anxious.
see, ever since my berthaw died
i'm here in this house by myself—except for my saints—
so
just to steady myself i say real sweet to her—real sweet—
"what you got there, baby sister?" and i'm reaching for her hand
and while i'm reaching for her hand
she starts to smiling, just a-smiling.
and then i open her little hand
taking her fingers one by one.
and what do you think is in it? she asks me.
what do you think is in her hand?

trying not to look impatient
"i don't know," i offer
trying push her along.
but she takes her time anyway.
"i don't know," i say again. "what?"

she smiles her own slow smile.
a knowing self-satisfied kind of smile—
pearlescent teeth beckoning like easy money spread out just inside the grasp—

leans forward for emphasis
hands poised on her two knees
fingers spread far apart.
and so i lean in too.

not a blessèd thing, she whispers
then laughs outright.
laughs near to choking so amused is she with the effect.
and when she stops laughing—
hand to heaving heart—
nods over in my direction
motions her chin up and over my left shoulder.
and when i look up and back
there she is.

6.
one two
—*mercy*—
and three four

honorée, she says
still tasting laughter at the top of her throat
honorée
this lady here come for a reading today.
why'n't you
take her on to the altar-room
where she can get her thoughts together, hmm?
it's when i stand to go along
that i see her smallness—
a child with an old woman's expressions
and old old eyes—
a child who takes my hand in hers as though we're friends and playmates
my right hand lightly held there in her left.
she looks straight at me with her old old eyes.
i try to smile the way grownups do with children but she's not buying
not today.

outside the rain is starting.
it will rain for hours now.
we have arrived apparently
at the chapel-room door.
the perfect little docent
pushes to the door and leads me through
having let go my hand stands there to watch me turn and look back for her.

she is watching me
she is watching me
and i can not see her eyes.

and this is the end / of the first part of the telling.

Regina

if you walk along the rampart past where it breaks into st. claude
one street back it takes up again.
a little farther on is frenchmen.
and frenchmen takes you nowhere:
not to the river
and not to the bayou.
frenchmen is a place you go to.
you do not walk along its length
going some other place.

but that is another tale
and more than is wise for you to know.

this end of the rampart
people like to tell
how regina went out to the backyard to hang the wash
and when she had strung her mother's bleached sheets
from one end of the yard to the neighboring fence
one hand flew to her head
and she began to dance
stomp barefoot
there in her mother's backyard
for anyone looking to see.

some say she danced till noon.
some say she danced till dark.
but they all say she danced—
a young girl
dancing the spirit beneath the clotheslines out back.
no one knows what grief or burden she's paid or borne because of that.

in this part of town
there is a tale for everything.

Memory No. 2

the day we buried mamma hangs in my mind
like a yellow-cotton summer dress on the clothesline out back.
what i remember?
how her sisters—the two who outlived her—
argued with me over everything:
the plain wood coffin
her body
the clothes i chose to lay her out in
the ribbon of blue silk wrapped loosely about her folded hands
which held no meaning for them
the mexican earrings hanging from her ears
the mass of grey hair i would not let the mortician dye or straighten
the nails shaped and painted that moony opal color she wore so often
and at the wake
the shameless way i touched her
holding
feeling
her hands and face
kissing her eyes and mouth
as though she were a lover
or alive.

that night you lay against me
your face pressed deep against the pit of my arm.
i rubbed your smooth neck with one hand.
you kissed my breast.
i thought of mamma
the yellow-cotton dress
blowing
hanging
on the clothesline.

ms. regina stands above me
above my naked body
laid out on the pile of burlap
filled with pungent roots
bruised herbs.
she steps around me in her stocking-feet
sprinkling scented waters
about the burlap and my skin.
through the long window panes leading up from the floor
i can see
the slates on the rooftops
take on the faint light of a late sun going down.
ms. regina bends and puts both hands
into the earthen vessel beside my head.
she brings out the red cloth
and puts it to my body
begins to rub
slowly
with a back and forth motion
my chest
my breasts
my sides
the soft of my belly
working her way
along the stretch of my body
singing in the same
sing-song voice she uses
for everyday speech.

i go back and forth
between a hard shaking chill
and the calm of yellow-cotton dresses.
when ms. regina leaves me
i am shaking almost to death.
when i awake the next morning
to the smell of thick coffee
and biscuits heavy with butter,
the shades are drawn.
i lie in bed beneath blue cotton sheets and comforters.
white towels and a wash basin await me
left in plain view
the way a woman ms. regina's age
would remember to place them.
i wash.
i peer into the looking-glass
tilted back against the window ledge.

when i let up the shade to see
there is ms. regina
in the backyard
hanging out the wash.

Faubourg Study: *Blood*

1.
the house sits at the corner
of st. philip and st. claude.
it is a two-story with a second-floor three-quarter gallery
stucco, painted old rose
faded now to shell pink.
all the women in this house are bleeding bleeding.
no one of us menstruates.
the youngest among us are still too young,
the oldest are already so long past it.
and those two of bearing age
are about as barren as the rest.

we are saints—blessèd—
and the people of the faubourg come
to pay us for our dreams.
today we walk the floor of the front-room
unable to recall
any time when it was any other way.

we are seven.
seven holy women seated all in a row.

we see the wind and rain before they strike
off in the distance
like a woman walking all flushed from market-day,
never stopping to speak or gesture or count her few spare coins.
we see the face of the storm to come
as sure as our own names written on the air.
we rouse ourselves and go inside.
outside the storm is whispering calling.
it calls our names each in succession.
the bleeding starts.
we are none of us ill or dying.
we merely bleed.

2.

hurricane waters crash along st. philip street
like a pack of jesuits on a ten-day mission.
stupidly i lift my skirts as if to save them from the rising water
a few steps later i stop to take my sandals off and toss them in my sac.
i do not look back.
i will not look back and up.
i know she is watching me
she is watching me
although i cannot see her

eyes.

—and three four
and mercy
three four and
mercy mercy—

and here they come
just as they always have
as we ourselves have come
when it was our time.

3.
it is the second day of the storm.
it is the third day of the storm.
we are all of us bleeding.
we bleed and bleed each one in turn
so that we are no help to one another.
the blood pools from us onto the hardwood floors
until we sit
having rolled up the carpets,
having bled through porch and house chairs,
sit about on haunches
heels pressed to our behinds
hunched down low on the hard hard floor
bleeding through the floor boards
into the ground
below.

what is the nature of the saint? the holy woman?
what does she dream when she lies down on her bed?
do her daily nightly visions follow?
does she sit down to table for cold fish and coffee each morning
like the rest of us?
does she never crave a man
heavy with the smell of the docks, the river?
does she bind up her breasts with white linen
washed soft beneath the hands of a good older woman?
has she *never* craved a man?
what does she dream at night upon her bed
having fed us all with visions through the day?
do her dreams then turn in and to her own in the night?
and when i pass her on the street
what is such a woman to me?

it is the third day of the storm.
it is the fourth day.
i go back to the corner.
i stand there in the wet and look up at the gallery.
the rain has shifted to a steady teasing drizzle.

the main door is already open.

the old woman comes to let me through the screened iron outer door.

she gets up from the floor and comes to me then and dressed as they are all in white.
and first, i see her eyes—and i am counting 2, 3, 4—
why am i counting 2 and 3 and 4

and then i feel the warm thin trickle down my inner thighs.

4.
we are only seven and always seven.
seven holy women sitting on a gallery in the sun.
people of the faubourg come
to pay us for our dreams.
we have no doubt
no one of us
that they will come.
they will come as they always do
as we all have come—
our dreams slung round like granny-bags each one of us in her time
each one her own caul heavy or weightless trailing
a thing of value
trailing in the dust.

from some window inside somewhere
i can see the sun begin to break inside the hard hard drizzle.
and then i see her eyes.
her young eyes smiling—*mercy*—
mercy smiling
up at me.

Morning

it is morning.
early.
we sit and smoke and watch the city come alive—
windows going up
the smell of hot frenchbread
of grits and eggs and coffee
fresh soap and mavis talcum.
next door ms. lonnie is cursing soon as the radio comes on.
and somewhere down the street
around a corner
somebody,
a child,
is teasing a dog.
screen doors will start to open and slam shut.
gaggles of small children in plaid or navy uniforms will
start their daily processions
to buses and schools and forbidden sweet shops.
you wouldn't think it
but there are so many men inside this city.
the old ones sit on porch steps
stand on corners
morning
evening
all hours of the day.
they talk or smoke or point with chins or fingers
and never seem to be waiting on anything.
the younger men
in dark pants or khakis
drive trucks, a few cars
the steamy red and cream-colored buses
that only ever break down in the awful heat of summer.

the younger men stop at their mothers' houses for coffee and hard frenchbread.
they sit or stand and stir the syrupy liquid about.
they talk about the weather
something a friend, some other man,
said or did or didn't do.
sometimes they hand their mothers money—
soft damp bills rolled into folds a little while ago.
and when they have no money to hand over
they laugh hardier
ask more questions
sit or stand a little longer.
and all the while
somewhere out of doors
neighbor-women are pouring out of houses in check- or flower-print dresses.
you can hear their off-beat chorus of good-mornings—
the blue and brown and yellow voices.
all day they will come and go
walking their own or someone else's children to school
themselves or some elder to a bank or a doctor
on their way to work or to market
to mass of ms. regina's.

i am leaning near the front porch steps with my old man.
my mother is somewhere inside
singing.

Faubourg Study No. 3: *The Seven Sisters of New Orleans*

intro:
take me to the edge of town
there ain't nothing left for me here
i said walk me to the edge of town, baby
ain't nothing for me here no more
                                    (as per the quintessential blues mamma)

I.
i do recall the day the last of them came into the city.
pack of run-down whores is what i took the lot of them for.
walking as if to come unhinged any minute,
and talking in that high-note,
that back-parish way.
was verde had to tell me
how he'd seen them
out far back as spanish fort.
give the mòn
two-three silver coins.
seemed they all were hungry
and most likely come down into the city
to pass.

well.
angelina like to died soon as she'd laid eyes on them.
pass for what? she screamed at verde,
pass for what?
just trash passing for trash
on account of a little yellow hair and tail?
got a pot to piss in nor a window to throw it out
and wanting to come downtown
trying to be something
they mòn neither they pòn
never was

course me
it was all the same to me
long as they didn't dot this doorstep.
and you might know that was just what they did.
had already got a dime or two of verde's
and then come here to me for rooms.
but that wasn't until after señorita put the lot of them out.

you should have heard all the commotion
once they took up there
living all on top one another—
which at señorita's
is the way everyone lives.
i tell you it was a mighty commotion
when señorita opened her mouth
for all the quarter to hear.
saying all how she couldn't have such carryings-on,
disturbance and strife,
in the house where she lived and worked
and ate her daily bread.
all how she just couldn't tolerate
such back-parish ways.
her place was respectable, *she said,*
no kind of cat-house.
a respectable place.
a house of assignation
on a good part of the rampart.

we later learned,
those of us who cared to know,
that the one called "baby sister"
had read señorita.
and of course señorita couldn't take it
and sent them out.
and where did they come to if not here?
right here.
and didn't even ask for verde
though he was the one helped them before.
no ma'am.
the one called belalia come straight up to the front porch
pushed the screen door to:
i'm looking for mister verde's woman
she called into the front room.
tell her i'm belalia.
one of the seven sisters.
and i'm standing in need
*of a good **clean** woman.*

2.
they were blood sisters every one of them.
grew up out in st. john's
the night the mother died
of the tumor she would not have treated
baby sister
whose given name was eulalie
took with a fit.
she made it out as far as spanish fort.
they came upon her
bleeding from the feet
from walking so far without shoe-the-first.
when they saw they could not force her to return to st. john's
they stayed with her there
and she convinced them to fast.
when the five days had come and gone
she told them not to worry.
their palms would be crossed with silver that same day.
a wagon would arrive to carry them in to new orleans.
and they would have food.
and rooms.
and not long after
verde barthelme pulled into view.

no.
they didn't come to pass or whore around.
they come to make a living
out of visions and such.
on the basis of eulalie's faith
they'd come into the city
as holy women.

3.
i swear they looked to me like any sisters might.
i'd offered them to come on in
but only belalia did.
the others stayed out on the front porch steps—
some standing
some sitting
all pressed close
around baby sister.
and when i saw up close
how she was right dark,
and one-two the others as well,
i turned my heel on all i'd thought about them,
on all angelina had been saying day-in, day-out.

those girls couldn't pass for mexican much less white.
and anyone with eyes to see would tell you
there wasn't a fast one among them.
i gave them the room verde's boy walker had died in.
i charged them a dollar and a quarter a week.
and angelina never uttered a hard word against it.

it must have been autumn or very well near it.
i remember the rains had started to come in to the city.
so it must have been early autumn
when the first one showed up
from bay st. louis
asking after a reading
with the seven sisters of new orleans.

4.

they lived on st. philip.
over there by that barthelme boy and his woman léanna.
never bothered anybody.
but then they never had to.
people came from all over.
bay st. louis.
all the way from memphis
to hear them tell
their dreams and signs.
had one called *m'dear*
she wasn't the mother of them though.
it had already been told how the mother's dying
was what sent them here in to the city in the first place.
she wasn't even the oldest.
she was the second
maybe even the third.
but they all called her that.

and the one who dreamed—
well—
they called her *baby sister.*

5.
i have heard tell of them, yes.
but i never believed the sister part.
people say they wasn't even *from* here.
come from way off somewhere.
foreigners or nations.
island people most likely.
reading and healing and getting full of spirit.
old-time hoodoo is what it sounded like to me
and i never did go in for all that.
roots and chamy bags and carryings-on.
and how come it's always got to be some *negro* woman
got to heal everybody?
what kind of colored woman *did you* ever meet
had time or inclination
to sit on a chair all day
dreaming and healing?
me, i had to work too hard.
and when i'm done over to the factory of an evening
them days i had children to raise.
had a man to feed.
had me a plot of ground i used to work out there in back.

yes ma'am.
misbelieve, collards, banana,
date palm,
melon here and there,
tomato,
sweet bell pepper.
even had a few camellia bushes out front the steps.
saturdays i baked all day
and sunday was mass and visiting the ailing and the dying
and supper for minor's people come noon.
and monday come another week all over again
and full-up with white folk besides.
no ma'am.
i never had time for no hoodoo.
and *seven* in one family and sisters too?
seven women all sitting on chairs
healing people from detroit and the west coast.

6.

going down into the city, baby
leaving it all far far behind me
i'm going down into the big city, baby
gonna leave all y'all behind
gettin' out before this mis'ry
make me up and lose my mind
i said i'm gone

7.

hail mary full of grace
   érzulie, mother of women
blessèd art thou
   there is truth to be made here
blessèd art thou
   dreams, mother, to be dreamt
blessèd art thou
   visions to be told
blessèd mother
   o! *lead me to the pathway*
blessèd mother
   over the barred footing
holy holy
   érzulie
      érzulie
   mother
mother
   mother of women

8.
lizette,
aurélie,
marie-claude named for father,
anne-louise, the blackest among us,
belalia who speaks for baby sister,
and my name is albertine
whom the sisters call m'dear,
and eulalie—
baby sister—
also dark,
who tells dreams and signs
gives out sayings and readings
but only when she must.
and only for the mother.

9.
you might not be from here.
but one time
some of your people
had to be from the city.
that's how we call new orleans, you know.
the city.
only city hereabouts.
some people think it's the only city worth knowing,
how would we know though?
we never go too far away.
no need to.
sooner or later
everyone comes to the city.
it's an old saying.

yes, daughter.
your people would have been from just over in tremé.
else you never would have got so far
packing that camera and your satchel of questions.
people round these parts don't tell much.
never did.
but you've got that look.
and that's the only reason they sent you here to me.
oh yes.
people'll fill you full of good food round our way.
and talk to you till you drop.
keep you all kinds of company—
but no one sends you to mother josefina
because of any of that.
and no one tells a *thing*
that is not for you to know.
so never mind about your questions
and just let me see what-all i might tell you:
i might tell you things you don't need or even want to hear.
i might tell you about your people over this way.
like i might tell you your condition.
but, daughter
let mother josefina tell you this one thing:
as long as you are here in the city
and whatever else you do
just don't you dream that journey.

10.
kind words
a place to stay
good company among neighbors who watch and report
and seemingly never intrude.
(and more food that anyone *living* can eat)
their hospitality is a way of teaching strangers
to know their place
a way of protecting the history
from falling into the wrong hands.
but you can not go without learning much
when you are not the stranger
you have so counted on being,
when you are really returning home.
you see too much; you feel too much
and you are always compelled to ask after even more.

the next thing, of course is you begin to dream—
that much i knew almost from the start.

II.

there is much i could tell you, daughter.
but none of it would satisfy your need to know.
i could tell you they died one after the other
the way ordinary people do.
i could tell you they passed into some vision of baby sister's.
i could tell of the long train of men and women
black, white, foreigners from i-don't-know-where
who beat their paths to this door
one after the other
looking for the sign
to fix their souls
or put their lives at peace
to heal their bodies or return some lost prize.
i could tell you how they changed my life,
the things i saw
or hoped or thought or dreamt i saw
the days i kept their company
scrubbing the floor where baby sister stood and walked
as she gave out
what few words she ever spoke aloud.
and i was glad to be of use.
a child
sent here by my father
because my mother died after birthing me
with the veil across my eyes.
he didn't have much learning,
god rest his poor country soul.
but he'd given me everything else,
schooling,
good clothes,
what love he had left, for mamma's sake.
so then he gave me the possibility

of the nearness to the journey.
oh yes.
there is so much you might learn from me.
all how i came to live in this house.
the house of the seven sisters.
though all this is not it.
the old house burnt almost down.
i saved what i could.
an altar setting caught afire
burnt away a good part of the chapel.
i saved some things.
that's how i come to be as you see me now—
saving and setting aside
so much that could have been lost.
and what you see here
is nothing.
as i said, i was a girl.
no more than a servant
and glad to be that.
glad to be of use.
oh, the many ways i was of use,
and to baby sister.
so much that the others never trusted me.
only m'dear had a kind word for me.
"baby sister wants you now" she said to me.
and i stopped all or whatever i was doing
and went into the chapelroom.
she was a girl, you understand.
like me.
she was just a girl without a mother,
just a little older than i was then.
you'd think they'd've understood, being her sisters,
and all so much older.
but no.
only m'dear knew or cared to know.
"it's time" m'dear said,
her voice like shallow water.
"baby sister wants you now"

that was how it was.

it was me she wanted to touch.
she believed i could feel what she felt, you see.
i was just a motherless child my own self.
only way i knew to be.
only life i knew was me and papa and saturday mass before her.
and you know, daughter,
it's true what they say:
a womanchild without her mother journeys a far piece of road.
the old folk say it
and i tell you it is true.
so it was me and baby sister.
me and eulalie.

i used to sing to her
songs she taught me from her mother—
which, i never did know.
yes.
i sang to her so that we could be girls together.
and more than girls.

and she used to read my dreams
"dream for me," she used to plead when i would go.
"dream for me tonight, josefina."
what could i do?
could i lie to her?
when we were girls like that together?
or else pretend some other dream?
no.
she wept like her heart was breaking that one day, daughter.
she wept so hard i wept along with her.
she walked the floor weeping
and me holding her up and weeping my own self.
because we both knew i had dreamt that dream, you see.

oh mother i am on the pathway
oh mother i am on the road
oh mother i am on the pathway
oh mother i am on that road
                    shallow water
                    shallow water loa-mamma
                    shallow water loa-mamma
érzulie
érzulie

        mother
    where i find my mother
        along the shallow shallow water

look.
the rains are coming in to the city
in no more than a week.
it never did take much of a rain to flood these narrow
streets.

but can you say it?
can you look at me, daughter
and say you have not dreamt that journey?
'course you can't.
come over closer, baby.
come where mother can touch you.

12.

oh it come up a mighty rain
and it blowed my house away
i said it come up a mighty rain
just blowed all my house away
couldn't find no place to please me
so i ride this lonesome train

13.
it has been three years.
and i have put away my satchel and my camera.
what notions i had
for some authentic study
some record of their lives.

the only family i have in the city
is uncle walker's granddaughter ava lee.
she sings at a new club on the rampart,
ANYBODY'S PLACE.

i will not seal or rent or close off any of this house.
and i do not lock doors.
i live among the sacred objects of their lives:
lizette, aurélie, marie-claude named for their father,
belalia who spoke for baby sister and bore her grudges,
anne-louise the blackest among them.
albertine whom the sisters called m'dear,
who organized their days,
who sought out josefina from her father's house
while she was still a child,
and baby sister: eulalie,
who on the basis of one solitary journey
made a living for them all
out of dreams and signs,
and died of clearly natural causes
at fourteen or fifteen or sixteen years old.

i live here.
i see few people
except for the handful of elderly neighbors
who still come to tell me their remembrance.
i listen to them all
recalling in single portions
josefina,
the things she told me
and her way of telling,
her early warning, still too late—
for me—
that song she broke into
of pathways and crossings,
ava lee
who consigns us all to the blues
impromptu
and unrecorded.
but i keep my own counsel
and i touch nothing
no one:

i want to walk a little farther
along the shallow water
i want to live a little longer
with my dangerous dream

House of Mercies

the structure is wood
painted white
a defiance of sorts.
but what you will notice
is the women
who enter late in the evening
and leave before daybreak.
what is it they hold
close to their skirts
so as not to have it taken suddenly away?
you will notice how different they seem
coming and going
collapsible women entering a wood-frame house
fully clothed
going quickly
even running
up the front walk
so careful when they leave
to close the rusted page-fence gate
looking about
some cherished article
almost covered in the folds of their skirts
bare feet slapping the paved sidewalk:

no woman swaggers or smiles
making her exit
from this house of mercies.

The House

I.

> *i can not hear myself*
> *over the hum of small-town heat*
> *and i am not getting*
> *the sound i need*

"we had to pay
to have the ice-man deliver then.
the girls would refuse food;
they liked to lick the ice so much"

> *in this place*
> *people create fictions around foreigners*
> *and 1954 cadillacs.*
> *where i come from*
> *there are stories to houses like this.*
> *you go inside for the first time*
> *it is stories come out to meet you:*

"it was years before we could afford gas.
we cooked in the fireplace.
there was a bloodstain right out front of it.
folks round d'abadie street
said she killed him,
said she put that meat cleaver in him
and cut out his heart.
the girls never fought too bad in that house.

they'd stand on the stair landing
looking down at the fire.
you could hear their child-talk:
     'say she cut it right out.'

     'fed it to her cat.'

     '. . . and watched him eat it.'

they do say she stayed in there with that body,
waiting for her people to come.
that stain never will move."

2.
"i have never been one for carrying tales.
he-say-she-say would easy get you killed
in assumption parish.
but to tell the truth
that augustine bears watching.
a child like that will bring turmoil."

"or sorrow,
for sure."

3.

loving this house
a neighbor-woman stands on the porch.
the weight of her words
bears into my gut:

"you'll have no peace in this house, neighbor.
you are like those women people read about:
the kind who cut and scream."

4.
more than a week it went on.
the sound drove the sisters crazy.
augustine's mother went into her room:
it was a mourning dove.
on the ninth night, augustine quite willingly
set it free.

when her sisters tired of it
the neighbor-women took it up.
        "nature"
        "nature"
she heard them say
from behind the false safety
of their close-knit porches.

augustine wore a smile bore no one malice.
her mother said she was just
peculiar.

   "like that noise;
   where'd it come from?
   her mamma says to me it was a pet
   a bird."

   "i tell you that girl ain't right."

   "my boy skite,
   he stopped her the other evening,
   asked her where she was going
   riding that de saix bus.
   that girl never said a word.
   and you know for a fact
   everybody round here knows my skite."

   "well.
   and no good ever come of jumonville.
   i can tell you for sure.
   but that's where i seen her myself.
   i used to go there to get read my own self.
   that's where i got read about my rodney
   and that milner tramp.
   no good come of that,
   did it?"

5.

"child, i can't help you.
but i can feel with my hands
and i believe you have a gift.
i can teach you what i know.
you can do what i do.
you can outdo me.
ask your mamma
to let you learn."

augustine shone in things
there was no need to shine in.
her sisters took up their tales.
they went to their mother;
it did no good.
"let her be," she said
"for jesus' sake
just let her be."

6.

"it was a monday morning.
we come downstairs
and found augustine scrubbing the stain.
she had the big scrub brush
suds everywhere,
working at that bloodstain.
she worked long after breakfast.
no one thought to stop her.
and late that evening
she went on to see doc, like always.
no one knows what he told her.
but when she come in
we were putting on dinner.
augustine went to the upstairs bathroom
and then she come down
and lit a fire in the fireplace.

nobody knows what he told her.

augustine stood in plain view of the kitchen.
she ate rat poison
and threw the box in the fire."

2.

mourning like a skin

Peculiar Fascination with the Dead

First you see the vision. Then you see
the woman who made you see.

light candles to honor the dead.
set flowers on the altars of the dead
which must be raised in your home.
wear the memory of the dead plainly
so anyone looking will see
how the decent do not forget.
speak of the dead
as though you thought they might hear
from the adjoining room.
keep mourning portraits
always about your home.
marry memory to the dead.
put silver coins in the corners of your rooms.
pray for the dead.
go into the tombed cities
along basin, canal boulevard, valence and esplanade;
carry flowering plants
bits of brown paper
smooth stones
the burdens of what time you have left
to honor the dead
as they ought to be honored.
live among your dead,
whom you have every right
to love.

part one:
it is 1969.
i go alone with my brother for the first time
to our grandfather's grave.
we search among the tangled growth.
my brother finds a skull.
i refuse to touch it.
he sees i am afraid.
it's dead, he smiles.
it can't hurt you.
i don't like the way he says *it.*
surely death
is more complex than that.
but i am twelve
and a girl besides.
twenty
thirty minutes
maybe more.
we find papa's headboard.
when the gravetender turns his back
my brother puts the skull
into the brown paper sack that carries our tools.
i look at him a long while.
he does not care.
he bends down
and begins weeding.

later
at home
when he pulls out his skull during dessert
our grandmother slumps into her coffee.
it's not papa's head, he offers in self-defense.
mamma stops tending her mother
to slap one side of his head:
get up from this table
and take that thing from this house, now.
i sweat.
my face turns cold.
catch your sister, i hear mamma order him
before she hits the floor.

some days later
i find the skull beneath the front porch steps.
i tell mamma.
she looks at me in disbelief
following me to the spot.
when he comes home
she takes him by the shoulders:
you are taking that thing back where it belongs
back where you found it.
say nothing.
tomorrow morning we take the bus to the cemetery.
don't you answer me back, child.
my patience with you
is wearing thin.

i did not take the bus ride that next morning.
who wants to see her mother
walking about
among the tumble-down graves no one cares for
and the gravetender in his overalls
pretending not to see
looking at your slender mother
in her straight garbardine skirt
pitchblack hair swinging down her back
sweat breaking out on her forehead
above her lip
even though everyone knows
it is always cool inside the cemetery gates?
who wants to see her mother
stop before her own father's grave
the favorite daughter
admiring the work of two children
learning to honor the dead?
i stayed home with my grandmother.

we play bingo.
she lets me win twice.
we eat black-eyed peas.
she looks at the clock a lot.
she makes us both hot toddies
and makes me promise not to tell.
i worm up close to her:
the smell of tweed
and sugared whiskey.
we climb into her double bed
even though it is still early.
we nap until they wake us.
mamma has brownies.
we agree to save them for the late night movies
she says we can all stay up for.
mamma sits on her bed
wearing only the blue slip
with the pleated bottom.
her skin is like new pennies.
she puts her hand to her forehead that way.
she lets me watch her
without snapping her eyes the way she sometimes does
if i stare too long.
i remember how she looked
after being in the graves all morning.

i was twelve years old.
it was 1969.

part two:
let the dead rest.
please.
she was our sister.
why must you always talk such dirt?
she was the one told you
about that damned husband of yours
but you had to hear it on the streets.
even so, you kept him.
she was your sister.
you will not speak of her that way.
not in my house
not in the house my dead husband built me
with his own two hands.

my grandmother alberta's younger sister
has a hump in her back.
it comes, they say
from all those years in the factory:
her slight body
bent over the sewing machines
standing the long hours into evening
trying to keep one eye on her husband
working on the mezzanine above:
the cutting floor
where the men earned so much more money
whisking our collars and lapels
from fabric and stiffening,
and the few girl-women who ran their errands
fetching new blades on command
trying to avoid
the swift dry hands
that ran up their dresses.
at least the decent ones tried.

part three:
the mourning portrait.
uncle son in his casket
dressed to kill.
features pulled tight across his skull
death mask of a self
that danced and cried
ate red beans and rice
made love to women
refused to marry
until he fell ill.
they never knew what killed him
a heart weakened by strong drink, rich food,
or lorraine's deep grudge:
some fix choking the life from him
as he lay half asleep in her bed.
if not her
then any one of the others.
we never will know what it was.

my grandmother kept the portrait.
the other sisters would not have it.
their younger brother
dressed in his best suit
—of which there were dozens—
some perfect white shirt,
almost his most handsome self:
the clear brown skin
with its waxy glow of death,
the grey silk pillow beneath his head
his greying hair cut close
brushed back,
the perfectly manicured hands.
they say they don't bury you
with shoes on your feet.
my grandmother said she had no idea.
she knew they buried him with his rings.
the gold watch and chain some woman had given him
did not to into the grave—
not from respect for his two widows,
but what need has a dead man
for the passing of measured time?

part four:
the people sit about like shadows of other people
lined about the walls
of the room we all have gathered in
to wake ms. munday.
i want to know how she will get up
if she's still dead.

the first three nights in the grave are the saddest.
only then do the dead know
they have left behind their families.
and there is no comfort
to bury such loss.
we sit with our dead the first night
to show we are not afraid to go on
and then we set them free.
we must not burden our dead.
those first three nights are carriage enough.
and we want to be well-remembered
even among the graves
the walled cities
of the dead.

my grandmother does not answer.
be quiet child, she says to me.
the dead go into the ground.

we waked ms. munday until midnight.
she did not rise up.
not even for rev. munday sitting at the foot of her casket
looking toward the back room
of what had been their home.
i thought she and death were the same thing.
even in life she had not been so pale,
that tarnished white
like bones a dog plays with in the neighbor's side-alley
but will not eat.
that is why white is a mourning color:
the spirit takes off
leaving no sign
of substance or color.

there is not much else i remember.
i fell asleep
across my grandmother alberta's thighs—
the smell of mavis talcum
and tweed.

part five:
mother lights the yellow votive candles
and places them all in a row
on the small altar
in the east corner of her bedroom.
she remembers the dead
with bits of paper
white carnations
a glass of water
one empty earthen dish.
she kneels without grimacing
and does not close her eyes.
i look at her back.
she is short-waisted.
the lowest edges of her black hair
rolled under
shine almost violet.
i watch her from the doorway.
i am playing with rubber animals.
they belong to my brother.
he does not want me to have them.
few cars go by.
you can hear people talking from the street.
rising to sit on the edge of her bed
my mother dresses her hair in mourning braids
crossing them over the crown of her head.
she secures them with bobby pins
the firm touch of her palms.

she turns to look at me.
they say her eyes are light
for a woman so dark.

part six:
i carry silver coins
in the pockets of all my clothes.
photographs of my dead follow me
to each new residence.
votive candles and st. john's wort
go near the head of my grocery lists.
i burn incense
sprinkle cinnamon out the back door of my home.
a great deal of the time
i find myself looking
for no good reason
over toward the east.
i judge lovers
by the heft of mourning
below their eyes,
picking my way through their sorrows,
handling the loose stones from which they must build up
the sturdy walls of their grieving.
i forget nothing
and carry the grudges of my dead
like bowls of ash.
i have never avoided
the tombed cities i was taught to tarry in.
and i have not let my dead lie.

you might say i have
this peculiar fascination
with the dead.

☦

Stones of Soweto

A Mourning Poem for Moses Nkondo

our recent dead have no shame.
they stand among the daily stuff of our lives
insisting on remembrance
attending the first signs
of forgetfulness or sloth
to damn us with their silence
the violent quiet the dead know
as no others do—
the holes they have left
in what we call our lives.

no. i do not forget.
part of me goes dutifully into the ground
where my father's own dust
makes its place among the hard
and equally silent stones,
down where you wait
for the heady remembrance
of other sons like me
who have yet to die.
how will you know me
—any of us—
from all of the others
calling out to their dead
among the clamoring stones and dust of soweto?

no, mother.
no.
now that you are also gone
now i can speak my small withered truth.
i do not believe in religions
no matter how well grounded
in the truths of our marrow
nor in final rest
—only the silence that enshrouds us
and gives no relief when i call out "mother."
only memory
—that is something like prayer.
and how will you tell me
from among all the other mourners
calling out to their dead
among the stones of this city?
how will i know you are not turning
ever turning to the cries
equally resonant
equally late
of other sons
of sons not yours
also folding dark arms upon dark hearts
oceans and oceans
away from home?

i sit and talk.
i sit and write.
i walk or drive the streets of new england and new york.
and all around me
death walks like a loose woman along these city streets.
down south friends tell me
the catalpa trees
bear heavy mottled flowers
out of season
and in the rain.
i am only one man
full of my own little words
and perhaps no great gift as a son.
it is true i am silent.
it is true i do not weep
or shout
or pray
or curse the lonely fates.
but i am only one man
lifetimes away
from all i have called home.
and my grief when it comes
is like a train whistle in the night—
if you sleep soundly
you will never know how it came or went
or how many souls it left standing
empty-handed along its tracks.
and anyway
the night is dark like me
and so soon gone.

i tell you mother
i stand worlds and worlds away from your rest.
i did not see your face in death
but your living face
i have carried in my deepest places all these years.
i can even say
that once i saw you cry.
i walked into your and my father's bedroom
only to find you sitting there
pools of tears
in your two cupped palms.
perhaps no.
perhaps it was not like that.
nothing like that at all.
but that was many years ago.
i was a boy.
and i had never seen you weep before.
nor does it matter why you wept.
you wept your tears.
i saw them.
i must have stood
—a mute fool—
some time before i looked away.
but that was many years ago.
i was a boy.
perhaps you yourself will not even recall.
but your living face, mother
i carry in my deepest places.

i stand on some anonymous bridge
above some body
of cold and moving water.
i do not smoke cigarettes or carry change
and so have nothing
to toss in.
from where i stand i see no reflection
save some vast and murky sky.
it could be any time of year.
i am not cold.
i stand and look across the water.
it could be any time of year.
i could be any man.
i am your son nonetheless.
i know your name.
i carry your face in my deepest places.
i do not believe in gods and their musings.
i do not believe
only in silence
and memory
that is something like prayer.
i believe in my own name
and the many clamoring stones
of soweto.

Another Time and Farther South

For Clyde R. Taylor, A Mourning Poem

in another time and farther south
i would give you ashes for your dead
clean white kerchieves of linen or hand-worked silk
spread crushed shell before you
and tell you to kneel there
and weep in dignity
like a man.
but these are times of strangeness; we are no kin.
and this cold dry air of your native northeast
can not tend such an aesthetic
as these gifts of mourning would require.
so who am i to tell a man i barely know or love
to kneel in the dust of pride and much remembering
weeping loudly for the death of a mother
that no memory of pain can take away
and no amount of sorrow can return?
can i say death is one more burden, friend
and we bear it with us into even this driest earth?
can i tell you there is no time passing
no fondness in the eyes of friends that will return to you
the life of the only woman to warm you in her belly
and give to you the very life and air you live and breathe
the blood that warms you
so much of what you think you know and have forgotten?
no.
these are words and stand for nothing more.
but i can say that in another time and so much farther south

i could have led you through the streets in ashes
one of several women bearing you along
to some sainted spirit-ground you could believe on—
a man who had lost his mother, still a son.
and we, the cluster of women
could stand aside beneath the palms
pressing roots of ginger underfoot.
watching you learn the lesson only death would ever teach:

how you can lose so much in life
and walk upon the earth a living man
wearing all the shrouds of mourning like a skin
and memory like a stone inside your organs
alone for all the rituals of yielding, giving up
and still walk home
finding your way among strewn ashes in the dark.

Requiem for a Chief

In memory of Big Chief Allison "Tootie" Montana, 1922–2005

> *Kânda n'landa: bankala kwènda; bankala kwîza.*
> *Kongo proverb: "Family is a channel: people go out on it; people come in."*

> *All of them people dead; but in my heart, I kept it going.*
> *—Chief Tootie Montana*

2.5 billion
science tells us
is the number of heartbeats
in the course of an ordinary human life.
and most of us anyway have only a little while
to stay.
till one day death comes dressed in white
and dressed to kill
carrying only his lantern and his own shroud
and just like that
we go—
if we're lucky
or mighty
or blessed.

sometimes
in spite of our selves
we do what is right and good for one another
or make some effort
but like as not we slip
and falter
and shirk.
and every year more youngbloods fall down
along the littered and illiterate city streets.

sometimes a warrior comes.
and then he goes.
and when he goes out
we sing his song.

if we are lucky
and if we are blessed
we will live to tell it
how
there is a city
where the chief was a true chief.
and as soon as death called him
the chant went out.
the tale went round.
and fourteen days the people told it
and fourteen days the people sang
until they were ready enough for the slow drum and tambourine
the final crown of gold
and the lifting up.
and when the storm held back
and the songs all turned to prayer
it was just too beautiful
for words.

it is not true.
it is *not* true:
his heart did not weaken or fail or give out.
he gave it to *us*
so that
somehow
two and a-half billion seems
a small small number
for such a chief
such a mighty mighty man
who gave to all our city
his warrior's heart
of gold.

For Charles H. Rowell, on the Death of His Father

1.
go tell them i have laid down my yard shoes
my house keys, my dead wife's handkerchief box
and the sight of my children
leaning at my face
in old photographs on the livingroom walls
and their voices saying
it was then
i saw it
he was with me in the field
we saw the brown dust when it covered the evening
all of these things:
i have laid them all by.

they are mourning me
and i am still a living man.

2.
my father stood in the field that evening
sifting the brown earth
through his turned-up fingers.
walking a little behind him
i was going through words in my head
testing how they sounded
in the empty expanse of the land.
he said something about a nephew
nathan or somebody.
i pulled on my cigarette
and watched him stretch his arm
across my line of vision
motioning over the field.

3.
my mouth is a barren plot of ground
a sand-colored silence
where my children stand hollow
over breakfast
two rooms away.
they discuss their mother
and the color of my urine.
they make these little sounds
eruptions i am not yet used to.
my death is in their throats and lungs.
they swallow hard before entering my bedroom.
my used body parts
are already in the grave.
i wonder can they see
how my soul is a grey fog
creeping the fertile land outside this window
to the left of the house?
but they want me to say something
because all my life
my name has been josiah.

4.
it is over now.
people are calling me long-distance.
writing on postcards
telling me how best to grieve.
they do not know that the young do not mourn.
they do not know that my hands are empty buckets
easily weighted to the ground with such stones.
they see me move both feet in succession
and rub my back with funeral lore.
etherine sings about *sweet peace*
others say *yes*
and talk of *going on.*
but then,
they have never seen the brown dustclouds
rolling over the rich alabama soil
on my daddy's land.

Requiem for a Tall Man

(for Thomas Covington Dent 1932–1998)

and so they took your heart
broken breaking poor strapped and strangled
took it as they'd taken dozens, hundreds before
and tried to feed its own life's blood back to it on the
sly.
who could have seen
beyond such clotted paths to loving
big enough if not for all the world
then surely all
this city
to run right through?
how connect
the many years of hurting
to be the thing you said you were?
to learn your own thing well enough to
have it
even a little
then pass it on?
on.
so they stapled you up the way they do these days and sent you home.
"i'm so glad" you offered from your hospital bed that first afternoon
"so glad i never really did anybody wrong"
and you were afraid
the way only a good man can be.

they will say that you were greater
wiser
hipper
even taller than you were
just to say
or to avoid saying
the deeper thing.
we loved you
far better than we knew or cared to know.
and you are not long enough gone
to help us through it anyhow.

there are tales the old people used to tell when the world was younger
more hungry
less fearful
of losing cool
of soldiers who came among us for a short time only
bringing peace.
does anyone here understand the proverbial moment of silence?
*can we not **always** be testifying?*
can everybody please just shut the fuck up about it?

death is a road.
and those we love and those we've loved not well enough
walk on it.
we carry them the little ways along we can
then stand aside
and watch them go
splitting memory and time
words like *asunder*
are useful in such moments—
slave ships in the distance—
centuries longer
nearer
than we care ever to have it said.

is it only we are older
more lonely and afraid
full up on casualties of living and the giving-up-ness of it all?

the people say your name
in atlanta and d.c.
new york and memphis
charleston, soweto, bayou goula and jackson
friends and near-friends
pleasure clubs and the holiest old dives
churches you never entered
except the briefest glance about
asking with that wayward ardent *need* to know:
are the people there?
*are the people really **in** there?*

juke-joints and side-alleys of despair
sidewalk bars and cafés
would-be variations on the same
are the people really in there
conjuring up your name
as if it meant something it never did
or could?
as if
conjuring *you*
somehow would bless their faces
sad, beshitted lives
and after all the rest
—much to your own belated dismay—
famous at last
in the *times-picayune.*

because we are here.
because sometimes sweet soldiers die foolishly in the middle of a summer's
afternoon
stricken from us like—*what?*—
between one ragged heartbeat and the next jive step.

because somewhere
dahomey angels sing into the night
where?
somewhere a koura plays cool round purpled notes.
and eternal dusk.
and the sweetest blackest coffee ever roasted over flame
flows *where?*
crazy laughter and footsteps and every face we ever loved.
and the river connecting every road.
fields of cane strong as bamboo
yielding.
fields of indigo, cypress and rice
stands of palmetto
savannas and midnight sky
black as your very heart
and half as wide.
and there is where the people are
there
inside
a love so terrible and sure
sure as all get-out
that saints *do* step in congo-time
home to their one true city
like soldiers
in times of peace.

Alberta (*Factory Poem / Variation 2*)

when my grandmother alberta was a girl
she worked in solomon's factory
alongside
women
who stood to stitch men's suits
to hang from the shoulders of white mannequins
who would not say *thank you*
for the any number of needles sewn through flesh
to put food on the table
to keep children in school
or a husband home
to avoid the indignity of government "relief"
to protect a mother or a father
from the old folks' home.

my grandmother alberta was a girl when she first saw
women eating small sandwiches
or bread dry-long-so
from the hip pockets of their dresses
as they stood sewing
because they were given no time for lunch.
women bleeding through triple-layered toweling
afraid to leave their machines the length of time it took
to wash and change the wadded cloth between their legs
afraid to lose the pay
solomon's sons doled out at week's end.
and more than once
a woman who had to go—
but not soon enough.
a woman sprawled against the white commode

the dark fluid slipping across the floor
and the two or three other women
standing guard against the door
hiding away the solution:
quinine and castor oil
to bring on the quick violent abortion
that might let you stagger back to a machine
to stand and stitch together
collars and lapels
welt pockets to decorate white mannequins
propped up in better stores
throughout the southern region.

she was a woman with a husband and children
by the time she knelt
between her own baby sister's knees
and caught the nearly full-term moving mass
felt its warm head in her hand
before she flushed it down the toilet
and wiped between galena's legs.
all kinds of things i saw and did she said
working in a factory of women

and it was no time
before she was promoted to floor-walker
freed from the stooping posture
of those women who stitched
heads down in silence
or singing across to one another
lyrics spun out above the hum of motors and needles.
often it was the threadcutters
whose bottoms bore into the long wooden benches

where they squatted gap-kneed more than sat
who tossed out a line
and it would come back
stretched by the heavier voice
of some woman who stood all day
wiping the oil from her fingers
into the blackened wood
of her upright atlas machine.
such a woman sent back a line stretched to endurance
altogether seamless
against the drone of motors
working at full pitch.
my grandmother alberta walked the boarded spaces between the women.
she walked.
she kept time.
is it any wonder she asks
as if i were to answer
is it any wonder
we sang like that?

2.
a great deal happened the year i was nine.
so i suppose i must have been nine the year my mother
not my grandmother
taught me to embroider.
i sat cross-legged on the hard floor
bunching upon the coarse cloth
that would become
dishcloths
tea cozies
for my grandmother
who surely had enough of one

and small use for the other.
later
much later
i learned to fashion
elaborately flowered pillowslips
dresser scarves
lace edgings she loved to store up
to show off to relatives
foolish enough to visit
during the long new orleans summers.
your mother does a fine stitch she says
watching me lift then re-set
the heavy iron over the face-down designs
as i was taught.
when i do not look up from my task
she offers at a lower register:
sewing is different
no one teaches you to sew.

3.
the men who worked the mezzanine
the cutting floor above
looked out across the vast crowded floor of women,
rolled up white shirtsleeves,
took white chalk in hand,
marking and cutting.
men's labor.
calling for a certain daring precision.
and higher paying
affording short breaks
to smoke or eat

to drink rc cola on the stair landing
to take time to look across the crowded floor of women
on the ground level
manufacturing blues.

4.
"we stood together.
we worked together.
we cussed old man solomon
and the day he ever set foot inside this city.
we cursed the cloth we stitched together
and the lives it cost us to stitch it.
we cursed the babies we dropped
and the men who gave them to us,
the bodies, our own bodies,
that held to them in the womb,
the conditions that dogged us so
and made us drop them
by choice or by accident
by long standing in heat or cold,
the perfect solution handed over to us
by the women we stood among,
manufacturing blues
for all we were worth."

these are the last words
the words my grandmother alberta
did not say to me.
my grandmother alberta is dead.
she can not speak to me further
of her youth among those women
her and her baby sister
down on the ground level
among their upright atlas machines.
she can no longer hold up at eye level
her slightly yellowed middle finger
sewn through the nail
the smooth even split
where the machine tore flesh and nail
and after all those years
the nail refused ever to grow together again.
my grandmother alberta is dead and buried
and reduced to ash.
i am her last remaining evidence:
the smooth
straight
seam.

3.

something about trains

Speaking of Trains

—for Moses Nkondo

South Train Study, Movement 1

in the early morning hours
when the building makes what few sounds it has rehearsed
during my brief sleep or absence
i move about
as little and as cautiously as possible
among strewn books and record jackets—
lyrics that tell of train whistles
of men standing alone
in vacant lots
men in the process of leaving cleveland
st. louis, d.c.
trains heading south into the night
trains that never return.
i toy with phrases like
cultural memory
canonization of despair—
i invoke rituals of loss and forgetting.

i do not sing.

i make this other sound
that catches the tissue of my throat like a bit of fishbone:
it dries there
and returns
in chorus with some country harmonica or bass guitar
a piano touched
by rude eloquent hands.
and i feel at the pit of my belly
the most critical essay of my career:

this year
i interrogate the blues.

> going down to the river / gonna take my own
> easy chair / and if the blues don't get me /
> i'm gonna rock right on away from here /
> that's why . . .

infra-blue:
ritual study in struggle.
i interrogate the blues
for something like fullness of meaning—
but there are codes here
dark men
and darker women—
and i feel in my own hands
the immeasurable buoyancy
of *am i blue?*
am i blue?

> went down to the railroad / laid my head
> down on that track / got to thinking 'bout
> my woman / snatched my devilish head back /
> wanna know how long . . .

in a new york barbershop-headshop
the older brothers talk trash
incorporate me into rituals
of loss and suffocation
desire and claim checks and umbrella stands
razor cut
trim-and-shave
pomade:

"what was her name?"

"man, i never did know.
but she only ever wore blue.

hell.
i just called her baby."

st. louis, chicago, d.c.
and the men stand vacant in their lots
in the process of memorizing
canonizing some moment.

> *in the dark / in the dark / baby, you and me /*
> *in the dark /*

like any other sensible man
i carry home that image
like i carry home my haircut—
incognito.
absolutely prepared
to promise things i cannot possibly give
if i can know her name
if i can know how she got away that way
in the dark.

i interrogate my senses
for the dark woman coded in blue.
like any sensible man
i work my way through traffic to the station.
she does not arrive.
evening trains
never do arrive.
i change my mind.
forget this city.
which of these women could ever remember?
which of these women
could be movement in blue?

it is evening.
i have my fishbone
and my hands on my belly.
i have my essay
and my evening meal.
i move about as little as possible.
the older brothers
and their infra-blue.
railway stations south to cities i will never see.
i have my ritual study in struggle-in-the-dark.
i have my dark code
painted onto the backs of my hands.
i practice
how i will say

"some questions
have more rhythm than others"

    repeat

    repeat

    offstage / enter woman in blue.

Movement 2: How to Meet the Train

i have a method
for meeting the train
no one has scooped.
i go with empty hands.
i go with my beard
just barely unkempt.
i stand apart from the wall—
never lean.
i do not smoke
or drink
or eat the salted nuts.
i have a method for meeting the train
no one has scooped.

missing trains all my life
at one station or another
i have become
a man who understands
the cries of whistles—
the process of waiting.

going to meet the train
i wear my city eyes
turn up my collar
uncautious—
still not reckless.
distant—
but not yet incognito.
you think you recognize me.
but oh the many ways i could tell you you are wrong.

Incognito: Woman in Blue

the streets are empty tonight.
i walk alone along this evening street
carrying nothing.
i have business in this street
i will divulge to no one.
i have some place in your dead remembrances
and i will not set you free.
you may not touch me
or speak to me
or discover my name.
i have these gifts for you.
you must accept them
without ever discerning
what they might be.

it is a hard business we bargain in here tonight.
and there is strange conju afoot,
brother.

("incognito—
woman in blue
walks—
past every known landmark
past every familiar thing
by which i might know her.
she does not stop
or change pace.
she does not look back.
she walks as if she had no hips
nor anything between them—
as if she had
no concept
of mercy.

in the distance
inside some one of these houses
someone is trying
to sing like sarah vaughan.
it is not raining.")

these might be any streets
we might find ourselves
in any of a dozen lonely, yellow-lit cities.
we might be kin or lovers
or any other sorry strangers
in any foolish, terrible time.
and around us,
the night,
the dark,
and the hungry yellow street lights.
watch your step,
brother.
remember:
i know who you are.
watch your step.
negro men in every time
negro men better and wiser and lovelier than you
have been known to lose
life and the dream of life
in safer streets than these

and just ahead
is the station.

New Train Study

I Like the Sound of a Train in the Night

—the short warning blasts
and then the long low whistle—
as an old man's appreciation
or disbelief.

the sound of a train in the night is good.
it fills the dreams with places near enough
to be got to slowly
through mountains
over major waters.
brings the past chugging again inside the night.
and we who sleep and dream
then are safe
our negro grandfathers forever riding the night to make it so
to buy our peace
the beds we turn so softly on
covers
the foods we eat or refuse upon awaking

our negro grandfathers riding out the night
making safe our merest dreams
some twenty, thirty, forty
years or so.

Train in the Night / 2

geography of unopened dreams:
a weightlessness purchased
on the spit-shined oxfords
of dark, lithe men
who heft and carry your
many burdens
traverse corridors of that half-century you have
forgotten
have never known
call across to one another
greetings low enough
hip enough
to form the safety of lakes
blue green brown hills—
country of the night.
salvation paid
in crisp white collars
jacket sleeves forever on the shorter side of wrists
service not so much seen
as
what?
and the hands themselves
lovely and unlovely armor every
shade—black plum brown golden blue
hands of musicians and of carpenters
men accustomed to get their learning in
between-car breaks
defender courier crusader post
weeklies of a darker world
15¢ a month however many years

periodicals of happenings
etiquettes of injustice
hands—nails groomed to dull perfection
buffed to show the meaty color just below
hair cropped closest to scalps
where grizzled grey is bound to make
young daughters more daughterly
young lovers more lover-like
daddies
daddies to the world
that sleeps and clings to dreams.

tonight i am dreaming
of the
dark men who muster
steel cold iron across the country
driving power from unseen pits

tonight i am dreaming of trains
and trains
and trains and trains.

and
anybody seen my
sweet brownskin?
anybody see my sweet brown?
tell her sunset glory's done greased the rails
and long tall daddy's back in town!

i want i want i want
oh a handful of gimme
and a mouthful of much-obliged

what's the story, pop
and *gimme some skin*
nothing but you sonny boy
*all **over** the news and post*

there are hills and mountains in this country you will never
see
rise and fall and rise night and day
kentucky tennessee virginia
nothing but mountains
"kentucky mornings really do shine shine translucent blue"
but night in virginia
gurgles up straight *across* the dark
early morning there you
"see half
above and half below the clouds"
our
trains all wind to slow tremoring chains
humming hills and waters of night places
black with soil
soil black with coal and tar beneath
beneath a night you never
live
to see.

Train in the Night / 3

this chugging cross the land between one major water and the next
my brothers' dreams are populated with geographies
migrations building one
upon another.
in the dark
the whistles all are sounding out the towns.

who lives who
knows such places in this way?
who are those men who stand to watch the trains come in past dark?
who shoulder all the weight of what inside their nights.
who are my brothers.

my brothers' dark dreams
(my brothers)
my brothers' dark dreams—
and so when i hear the morning train
it does not move me

i crave and need
—something in my history requires—
the longtime coming of some train in the night.

4.

little history, part one

Qu'on Arrive Enfin

(a tale in-progress)

I.
and so we arrive at last in our native land—
the earth itself marked by slavery.
up there, in the open air, the stink, the hot funk of hot blood
the rowdy rebel-niggers of the past.
funny, no?
how we always return to this—
the city, the life
that slavery built,
tales altogether invented
as told by historians, founding fathers, the church.
but we are sick and tired of lies, dirty tricks and fraud,
we are sick of tales and of historians
sick of indigo, tobacco, rice and rum
we are sick of king-cotton and sugar cane
sick of it all
and can only wish hard-hard-hard
that the lakes, the bayous, swamps large and small
will have swallowed it all
flooded
erased it all.

but then
we don't bother about this, really
because there's always (the chance of) hurricane.

therefore, down with the dealers in blood and in flesh

long live the conquering hurricane
long live the leveling swamp
long live the rowdy rebel-niggers and the bad little niggers as well.
let there remain not one single plantation to reek of the stench of roasted flesh-and-blood.

2.
and so i ask myself,
what would suffice?
and my answer,
nothing. not a single thing.
as long as ever i live nothing nothing nothing shall ever suffice it.

3.
used to be
a good while back
used to be
they'd chop heads over far less.

and how many bloody heads *would* have rolled back then?

        and so every time we hear the word "creole"—
        or better still "le monde créole"—
        the fetid breath of the slavers and their lesser merchantmen

        and the great stench of their women taking their little whores'-baths
            only every three days or so

and so what?
what's it to us we ask ourselves from time to time
a thousand times over
what's it to us?

used to be
used to be
once
upon
a time

4.
and i can not   quite   fathom it

all.

5.
what then is history?
hardly even fable
hardly even myth—
nothing but the lies repeated by masters and their henchmen
nothing but lines repeated ad nauseam
in order to memorize them well enough
in order to entertain themselves well enough
until time for slashing the throat of one of their negresses
        only after having fucked her good and raw

oh it's the factories
the accounting-houses
over there
just along the river
where they produce
neither grain nor sugar nor anything else—
the "social science" of slavery

Répétez s'il-vous-plait
Répétez s'il-vous-plait
        Tous à la fois à la fois à la fois. . . .

Slaves to the City

we stand in line to receive our daily bread.
it has the taste of sand
like so much else in this country
where there is no sand.
we move along the red-bricked streets
all of one piece.
we stop from time to time
to stare at buildings.
we do not know
have never seen such riches
and such places—and so many—
for the storing up of riches.
we are numb.
we move about together—all of one piece.
we stand.
we stare.
we eat our bread of sand and then move on.

where are the young
the children
the very old
our holy men and women
and our saints?
where are our sacred objects?
the little gods to carry on our persons
now that the great god sleeps?
we do not ask these questions of one another.
we do not dare.
we know our own small piece of truth each one of us.
nor do we share such truths.

we look into one another's eyes and faces
read nation, gods, wars.
we ask ourselves who will betray us today and whom we shall betray and
for what cause?
we do not ask the things we need to know—
we do not dare.

we eat the bread of sand.
we move along the red-bricked streets
stare into faces—
nations, gods, and wars.

The Business of Pursuit: San Malo's Prayer

A Ritual Poem for J. B. Borders IV

I
you walk the high road
between this land and the other
this dream and another
and are not free.
displacement
is a thing you know
at least as well
as your own good name.
a thing you have known
since setting foot on this man's shore
since taking your place
your woman
your house
on the high ground
on that man's high road.
or so you've been told.
      (and we've all been told
      —those of us young and sleek and determined enough
      not so very unlike you
      as the others would have us think)
so you have been told.
      (or thought
      or hoped
      or dreamt you knew all along)
your dreams run all the same these days.
in your vision
the heads are bloodless on their poles
mask-heads laid aside in their season—
eyeless, sightless, speechless things.
i stand outside your dreams
a hundred changeless years later.
i see your slightened and imperfect heart

—heart in a basket—
a bushel basket filled up with yams.
i see you braving the dark night of your dreams
and dutifully engaged
in the business of pursuit—
o great o great o great
deceiver.

i see you dream among the quiet known to be final.
i see your dream descend in calm when all is done.
i see your ungloved hands
and your eyes that look away in the opposite direction
—it does not matter—
i see you as if from so great a distance
i can not say
"he is coming
or going"—
i see only your form.
perhaps it is all i am able to see
—and so unlike any other form and perfect—
i lean forward in my desire, my prayer
until the roots fall from my head.
you are but gone.
i take my men, my women along the river road.
we go a-hacking and a-slashing
our bloody ungloved hands a-steaming—
we taste your freedom, luís congo.
your dying prayer,
your dying prayer,
brother.

2.

the night is a bastard gleaming
a leaning
a steaming
and full of questing.
at some point we all go questing in the night.
i say at one point it is all the same.
at some point the silence deepens.
the dark deepens
looses itself upon the city
—remorse
desire
regret
possibility—
the dark comes and shuts down upon us like a window
—the single
steaming
solitary
night—
i say it is then that we act.
i say i am afraid.
and i admit it.
i stand before you, beside you and afraid of my own truth, our truth.
afraid to lose the night loosing around, upon me
deepened
seamless
and silent
ici-dedans
com' peur
and cornered like a dog
in the heat of pursuit.

in this moment
i call my prayers about me and i act.

3.
the night is long.
the night is dark,
altogether seamless long and dark.
your eyes like mine make into gaping pools of unrest.
and yet you are brave. brave.
this is *our* darkness.
our night.
we have grown lean with much waiting.
we toss aside the make-shift covers like so many flags.
we bare our teeth and glisten—
our truest selves.
we pick up the bushel baskets of our hearts
a-slashing and a-hacking through the dark.

4.
big river
big muddy
big muddy shining water.
there are saints and spirits and loa without number.
i lean back on my heels looking out across the water.
i hold your traitor's heart inside my own, luís congo.
i do not see them coming
but i know that they are.
and this is how i know your hundred-year secret:
you must have had your vision
as i am having mine of you now
the emptied sockets
the eyelessness your own doing
blinded as you must have been, congo-man
by the mulata, the first gold-piece they gave you,
the house standing up above the rest
on higher higher ground.

you pressed
your lips and teeth and tongue in the service of your white masters
—the lot of them
and only one of you—
a slave at heart for all your wealth, they say.
i say different.
i say the traitor's heart is long and wide and deep as any other's.
what do you say, señor? m'sieu?
what could you say to those your brethren in the flesh?
could you say that you were special?
or saved?
could you say, "là, i see you in the sightless dark
coming with your evil down the white man's road?"
could you say you saw the river road, the men, the women
their elderly and children and those with child?
could you go before your own dressed in the white man's fine thin clothes
bearing your bloodshot eyes
your caul in your own bloodstained hands?
the road, broken, mending
and where it led to in the night?
o, i know you now m'sieu congo
brother, kindred
        mo vous connay bien fort
you are here among us now.
tonight, even as we pray and call and beckon.
among just so damned a crew as we you got your treatment
—revenge, respite, the holiest of reckonings—
        ici-present m'sieu congo, je vous sense
you speak the right languages.
you have your proper tongue, as we say in butcher-spanish,
but it is i, i
san malo, have your tongue.
i have your very own bushel basket.

and i say the dark is long and very very deep.
i do not see them coming but i know they come.

    o señor
    m'sieu
    je vous connais en fin
    et avec chacun des blancs je fais tué
    en fin je gout ta sang nègre
    en fin mo mo trouve capab' di'
    c'est mo, congo
    c'est mo vous voyé à la rue de la rive
    congo congo

your hundred-year vision is true at last.

    c'est mo

my head towering above the others
calling to you from atop this high ground:

    o petit-coeur si nèg' et si souffrant

give the white man in all this tumult at least his due:
when the blacks fell upon you on that fated day
he did not even stop to tighten his little bag of coins.
does not the proverb say, my brother:
when you must kill the snake
cut out also his tongue?

and who knows
that in another hour and other skin than this
—blood of your same blood that i am—
i would not have done the same?
only i and the great god.
my head goes up on the pole just as you decreed.
even so, m'sieu congo
in spite of treacherous blood
bushel basket and the like
my tongue is mine
and black as night.

5.
i say it is all the same.
i say there are angels
black angels
congo angels
free black congo angels
all singing the same songs
one hundred, two hundred years.
how free can any of us have been?
how different is the traitor's heart than that of any slave?
and how free?
i say luís congo looked out from his highest tower
        and cursed the dark, the land, his own slave-heart.
i say he saw them with their heads jammed to their poles
        and spat into the wind and cursed the night.
i say it is no small thing to betray one's own.
i say he had a vision and a lust for life as deep as any slave's.
but i can see them
—angels—
        in the middle of the day
        along the river road even as we speak.
i call the names of my gods
        —damballah
        papa legba
        yemanjá
        ilê fa ne wô—
i say when the moment comes
and the eyes are fully open
it lasts for but a second and then we are done for.
i only know the histories, the myths
what others tell me
and what my gods say to be true.

one other small thing:
i have never been to the chapelroom at ms. timotea's.
but when i go
i set my light on the altar of san malo.

The Head of Luís Congo Speaks

congo, tiamca, colango, matinga
bambara, nago
senegal, creole
i am the head of luís congo
and i speak for him
lying
burnt and rotting in some farmer's field.
and you
you may chant and shout
and dance about your bonfires on the levees.
and drink your aguardiente till you burst.
drink up until your eyes shine liquid.
and you will never have the vision that he had.
will never see the world as he saw.
what are you in the end
        but a wretched lot of slaves?
the lot of you
slaves
in an alien land
under the rule of a pale, slight and ghostly and alien man?

you laugh
you drink
and for a moment
your pain is gone.
but i am here to tell you:
it is not over.
a thousand thousand betrayals hound you
among even those of you
dancing on this very water.
it is not over.
he is only dead.
he is not yet through
with you.

THE HEAD OF LUÍS CONGO CRIES OUT FOR WATER

agua
agua
agua—
if there is among you any congo man
any man with but a grain of pity in his soul
give me a drink of water as i die.
but look
look they cry out in their festive voices
the head of luís congo
it speaks
it begs a drop of water
the head of the great murderer
our torturer
the head of luís congo cries out for water

THE HEAD OF LUÍS CONGO WEEPS

olurun   bon dié   mystère
here am i at the crossroads of death and life
i look out across a standing water
to the land of the dead—mpemba—
where i can not enter whole
and weep:
o mbanza kongo
where are you now?
i look and look
but i do not see
o mbanza kongo
i search but i can not find out
the streets of my ancestors
nor any relative to receive me
o holy mountain
high ground of my striving
source of every drop of blood upon my severed hands

what is to become of me
wasting in some petit farmer's field
severed
rotting
burnt almost to ash
o sacred mountain
is this the doing of my two hands
and where are they now
olurun bon dié mystère
how am i fallen
now that my head is mounted on high?

THE HEAD OF LUÍS CONGO CALLS FOR HIS MEDICINE

o great god   good god
where is my healing powder
the balm to soothe to cleanse anoint and clam
my head
my heart
my two strong severed hands
crushed beyond recognition
and burnt to solid ash?
bon dié   olurun
do not let the dogs
the crow, the beasts of the field
do not let them feed upon me.
mystère   mystère
where now is my little pouch
my paquet d'medecin
my healing bag?
where now are my banganga des mystères
who cleaned my head and heart and hands
and told such great things for my life?
where is my little bag
my faith
my medicine from this evil day?

silence! all of you, silence!
i tell you i am the head of luís congo and i speak for him.
enough
enough
enough.
mbanza kongo rises in the distance now.
she rises but i cannot see her heights.
she rises but my ashen feet cannot find her golden paths.
she rises and i stand on high
blinded to the glory i have set before my ways.
enough then.
it is true.
i have killed.
i have captured.
i have tortured.
and when i could not kill or capture
i maimed as best i could.
at my hands
at my very words
men, women, children
the agèd and those with child
fell down in heaps along the waters of the bayou.
many a soul
from many a nation
did i send on the watery mpemba way.
my pockets my house even my bed
were lined with gold
white gold
yellow gold
the gold of earth's roses.
and with every golden death among you
my house of gold rose higher and higher
nearer and nearer
the land of the ancestors.
and i became

every day
closer to their way.
and all of you—
congo men and mongrel nations alike
all of you
lived with the very intimate fear
of my good killing hand.
it is all
all of it
most certainly true.

THE HEAD OF LUÍS CONGO HAS HIS LITTLE SAY

congo tiamca matinga
colango bambara senegal
negro creole and more—
it is a good thing to live in fear of a mighty man.
it is a good thing to cross the water of death
being sacrificed on the altars of the king.
i came as you came
a minor man
crossing not one but two deathly waters.
and with every one of your heads
the gold in the seams of my pants
the gold in the posts of my house
the gold in the four corners of my field
the gold between the jambes of my mulata
the gold in the waters beside my great house grew
and grew
and paved the road—ever higher—to my greatness.
and what if i made myself a king?
this is a strange land.
a nether man's land.
and it is a good thing to be hated and feared—
is it not—
in a strange man's land.

it is true
it is true
it is true:
i captured and i killed and did not look back
and now i am captured and killed and cannot see farther.
but i did not take from you your healing medicines.
i did not take from you your human qualities.
i sent you—every one of you—
whole to the ancestors
and now you stand behind the walls of blessed mbanza kongo
laughing in your teeth
cursing the demise
of a mighty man
who helped you from your lowly life bondage
along the great mpemba way.
a curse for the peace you have in that great city
and i languish.

THE HEAD OF LUÍS CONGO BEGS A FAVOR

i am the head of luís congo.
and i have one small request from him.
if you cannot bend to give me back my medicine bag
then burn it with my ashes.
if you cannot lift up my eyes from where they droop along my cheeks
if you cannot lift them
so that i can see the great god
so that i can see the great city i will never enter whole—
i tell you
i am the severed head of luís congo.
i speak for him—
in the name of the fear and hatred you once knew of me
give me please
i beg of you
a bit of your cool
        fair
        water.

DOM-TOM Primer

les DOM
les TOM
le beau patrimoine

les dom
yé les tom

there is a certain kind of woman
who offers herself like an eden
and so one does whatever one wants with her
one does whatever one can with her
so long as one pays the bills
or at least signs the receipts.

there is a certain kind of land one walks on
without the least sense
of even being in this world down here.
they usually produce
bananas
pineapples
wonderful spices
all sorts of foods
sweet and peppery—
exotique—
they have names like—

well, they don't really have names so we have to name them.
and once they're named
we write them on maps of the conquered world

the vanquished world

and because we're humanitarians
we begin civilizing them.
and because we're interested in their good
we have to humanize them.
and to really humanize them
we have to study them,
anthropologize them
and to really study them—
and because we're such humanitarians—
we have to fuck them.
yes, to really humanize them
a good fucking is what's needed.
and all the while we're fucking them
we're also giving them lessons in civilization.
because we're humanitarians after all.
and that's good.
oui c'est bon
it's good to have that sense

of fucking
a whole people
a whole world—
oui—
to have the sense
of never enough
but then we've got to finish
got to conquer, vanquish, master
conquer and vanquish and master
because if not
if not
we'll have to sign the damned receipts.
we'll have to
because we're very humanitarian after all.
but one of these days
some woman's going to come carrying iou's.
and that's how we make
the *DOM*
the *TOM*
because it was *si bon*
that almost-ancient fuck-session
the DOM
the TOM
the héritage
ya-bòn
ya-bòn
comme ça
et ça
so that it's never finished.

O—les DOM

les TOM

comme ça

le patri—

moine.

2.

and what if one of these days
what if one of these days we were to finish with all this dom-tom-foolerie?
what if we decided to give up the taste for bananas and pineapples?
but what for?
all the best colonies are already taken back.
all we can do now
is *eat* the fruit of our labors.
it's not exactly easy civilizing the whole world like that—
or almost the whole world—
britain—
though no longer "great"—
played her part as well.
oui.
for back then, the world was so much bigger than today.
now there's nothing left.
it's over.
the world today—ruined—
nothing but minor countries, all pouting.
they're all finished, all of them.
and we
we eat some few pitiful bananas
and dream of lost years.
and so we have to eat them.
gulp them down.
swallow them whole if need be.
absolutely.
and if it were up to me to decide
i'd pass some new laws
so that the french
would eat bananas
every
damned day.
comme ça.

Regarding the Intermediate Travels of Cristóval Colón

i loved my father and my father loved me.
but it was never my dream to be a weaver.
i saw the bright ships sail
nor
do i know the first time i heard the word *spices*
but in that word
was magic
and gold
and more than gold
more than adventure
for there lay fame
bright and simple
as a clear day for sailing.
it was never my aim to be only a sailor.
nor was there nothing for me
in the turning out of cloths.

san salvador
marie galante
cap haitien—
such lands.
my own italy
even sea-going portugal
what did they know of such dreams?
mine was a soul already inclined
to greatness.

and when i went into the church there at la rábida
and looked upon the emblems blazoned there
i knew i had come upon my rights
and that good and catholic soldier isabel
could give more
than all the known desirings of
this heart.
and so i went to work.

my father was a simple man, a weaver.
he never could know the pull and heave of my heartstrings for the sea.

spices.
that was all my dream.
spices and the sea
and my name writ large in the great and handsome book of history.
will they recall, do you believe, how i all but alone, all alone really,
invented the *notion* of admiralty?

o seville city of a merchant's dreams
city that was my undoing
city that never was
and i shall have my own city said i to my brothers as a boy.
laugh if you will
but i shall have my very own city
streets paved in gold and every spice and peppered thing
and i will share with you if only you help me to find my way
out on the sea.
yes the sea is the only way to achieve the unknown lands.
laugh if you will.
laugh if you must.
but help me get my way upon that sea.

and so began my life as a navigator.
a boy of fourteen i was
and ripe with it.
already a mariner at trade before i was a man.

and if the sea cannot make a man of you then nothing will.
for she is a hard mistress
and brooks no infidelity—

o santa santa fé
was all my prayer in those days—
i cannot tell the hardships that she taught me.
i would not tell you if i could.

and then i read old ptolemy's cosmography
and learned to gaze the stars.
then i was sick with it as i never was sick before.
then planetary bodies made me hunger
just as the sea had made me thirst.
and i was mad for it
mad
and right they were to say it
but not in that manner.
what *can* they know of such dreams such hope?
land and sea
and land and sea
and everywhere savage hordes
half-naked gleaming
gleaming sweating reeking of humanity
and i lord admiral of those seas and more
who gave themselves to me
and gifts and foods besides.
who among you would not round the whole wide globe to be a king
where never man had ever yet set foot?
and pagans looked upon you as a god come from the sea?
and concubines of every heathen sort
swoon into death after bedding only some few times?
or else bearing onto the earth legs spread apart without a note of shame
and from the bloody mess of their loins a bastard son or daughter
heaved upon those dying breasts for some last glimpse?
worlds i tell you

worlds vaster than this strip you call the civilizing world.
such things i have seen with my own eyes.
such babes i have dandled and cooed.
who are you to judge me in the end?
who have never stepped beyond your fair genoa or minor tongue-tied lisboa?
who all will die some day of old age on a hard chair for your throne?
in spain they call me cristóbal the great.
my seed is scattered over islands you will never see.

    there was a maiden
    and yes i venture to call her so although
    she was a true confirmèd heathen and right proud
    her name some bright vexation of syllables she tried to teach me laughing
    but i had other uses for my time and hers and named her isola.
    isola
    daughter of that pagan prince—
    o isola of my broken seed
    and i will die never knowing the brood you carried in your loins for me
    and only lady dona felipa for my compensation.

for such is youth:
marry well and bring forth catholic sons.

when king affonso wrote to me
he did counsel me thus.
and i obeyed.
and i obeyed.
and not one piece of portugal's gold ever crossed my out-turned hand.

yes such is youth.

around and around the world
and still i am longing for my city
genoese in my heart that i am
and woven of thick hardy stuffs
i carry on
as
even now
bright ships
bright ships
i close my eyes
and still the bright ships beckon the while
to farther and to ever farther seas.

isabel and her father confessor and their king—
it was they who made me admiral
sovereign of all the seas
after the goddamned moors had cost me years of revenues.

17000 ducats.
a great sum to me then.
and came a time i tossed as much in trinkets
for the favors of a good and catholic king.
colonies
whole peoples have been named for my discoveries.
genoese you call me still?
no gentlemen.
you do not know me.
you do not know me and shall not judge me
ever.

around the world
around
the world
and no i never did find my fabled city.
she would be
cast in gold and in copper
she would be redolent in ointments and in spices—
dark savage womb of the world my sea—
and i would name her isola
and gladly die within her walls

an old man i am and do not expect to see more in this life.
i am an old man.
at night i lie upon my chair discomfited and watch the heavens.
some nights they do not come to let me watch them.
and then i dream a young man's dreams—
for i would name her isola.
yes and i would name her isola.

the land we called yamaye
gave riches in metals and produce and spices and more besides.
and they had only to subdue
my father, prince of the caribs
a seafaring people of great will and character and beauty.

they say that when my sister saw the stranger
she begged our father to give him to her as a gift.
and being a prince of good wisdom he would not.
but my sister was spoiled and fêted and the daughter of the prince.
what was to be done with her?
and so he gave the savage to her for a plaything.

and now here am i—guardian of the waste he strewed among us.
descended from the gods from the part of our mother
she chose to soil us
all of us with the stink of that old foreigner.
and she gave to her daughters bright foolish names—
marie galante, dominica, navidad, juana, española—
gibberish he cried out in drunken rages,
and she drunk with him
lurching from tobacco and aguardiente.
i see her even now
my mother's daughter
no better than the whores they tell of in those lands
the two who ever did return alive—
ironical that she
should live to see them spread out dead before her—
daughters every one—
and she persisting alone and in pain unto the end
the foul-smelling sores he gave her oozing down her legs.
at least she let him name her isola
so that perhaps we will one day forget how wide
the daughter of the prince
did spread her legs
to populate these islands
in the highest hours of the sun
while the gods were drowsing.
who would believe that
same disease that turned her womanhood to carrion
would also take away her sense?
"my daughters will be tutored at the court of the queen of expaña!"
she was heard to rave some nights.
i heard her myself
and did not move to help her.
let her stew in it i heard myself curse her.
and felt no shame.
and went instead to comfort our father
who was taking a long time to die in those days
of the sickness in his
soul.

the arawaqi were our younger cousins by marriage between the gods.
and had i not been so desirous to put them in their place
i might have seen what the yxpañaro was plotting at my kingdom
but i was distracted by their impudence
as well as by the complaint of my elder daughter
who would go on until she had her way.
and now she is all but perished from it.
and i have seen in my visions
how i too am dying
slower than a
man of my stature
ever was meant to fall.
as the arawaqi say
the gods are making great feasting on my livers and my heart.
and i have come to the end of days
and now must ask my younger daughter
to set me free.
every day i search her eyes for it.
and every day she shields herself from my sight.
is it love that binds her from the quest?
or hating desire for vengeance?
for foolish as was guantanamexe
as serious is guanaguahana.

surely no man of my stature ever was
meant to be brought low before those others
whose fathers served my fathers
in the oldest house of the gods
before there was time
or the history the yxpañaro wept so for.
my soul is too great
to fall so low.

the day i cut the heart out of my father and ate it live
was the day i became the warrior of my own soul.
and when i held my sister's portion out and she refused it raving
there was not a moment's pause until i put the machete to her
and threw the rotting shell of her from the mound.
they call us flesh-eaters?
i will show them the better.
for i have consumed the breaking heart and gizzards of my old father.
they were pierced with fibers of repentance and remorse.
it has made me valiant.
and it has made me pure.

now i am sitting squatting waiting the stranger's return.
now is the time of sacrifice and of destiny.
now i wait to see
another ship of strangers
carrying other evils from other lands.

i squat in the shadows of my green kingdom
guanaguahana
last daughter
of the last lord
of the guanahani
of the race of the gods.
and around and around
this old old world
the bright ships sail
the bright ships sail
bright ships
sail.

History

But I am tired today / of history, its patina'd clichés / of endless evil.
                                        —*from "The Islands"*
                                            Robert Hayden

and so we begin again our weary wearied and wearying lessons
because we have not learned them well enough.
only this time
without chanties about some ocean-blue
because for us
all oceans are forever red.
and we begin this time without the head and finger count
for what's the real measure of human loss
once figures climb into the tens of tens of thousands
multiplied by however many ships debarking from however many nations
to archipelagos of death, to continents of doom?
and still for all that chatter
gorée persisting into the red and golden sun
its few hundred or so inhabitants
making the daily ferry run
barely even eye-ing the western born
borne on across unroiling waters—
and boys are playing at games
innocent as all of time.
time and even more time is what has dullened us so.
for we are tired of lessons.
and yet it is to lessons we must go.

the looming sea is all about the wide wide world.
and it is wide
oh yes it is
the world is wide and wide and full of evil ides.
and the history of the world if we would tell it
would strike us all down dead upon the spot marked
with
its greenish stain like money in the poker-men's upturned pot.

oh and oh and i am weary with it all.
and here is yet another castle
another monument to look upon.
and docents with their sad or singing eyes—
the sharp accentuated hush that follows as they speak
men fingering chains and such
and women who will not turn their eyes
and children who look about beneath the words that take so long to tell—
the history of this world which if we tell it straight
will kill us all before we even taste the smell of even the most rudimentary hate.
on with it then.
then once and once and oh so long ago.
we can only tell so much at any telling.
we have lives—such as they are—and other work to do
and can perhaps only stand the telling of this history
in parts one and two.

in bambara and shango
wolof and peul tshihiba twi éwondo
in sara and sérère
in toupouri hausa mandara boulou
in yoruba kinyarwanda and ki-kongo
and all the languages around the hardy cape then
let us tongue and tongue as the aperture of the hardiest of the *old-line* trumpeters.
and this time
let us try for once to get it right.
and this time let us tongue it deep and well into the night.

and bring me now the bones of diogo cão
and bring the shroud of pope nicky the v^(th)
bring me the cape of old victor schoelcher
bring me the bastards
and let me have my way
and let it last until i've earned at last my full pay.

(the sun
bright disk cast against the sky
that shines without warming ever
wasted gold set against blue skies that are not mine
nor ever will be.)

o são tomé
o são vicente
o cape o cape of all good hope
elmina and cape coast
île de gorée
cabo de delgado
fort osu

all of them *"ages ago / last night / when we were young"*
shame   shame of ghana
thirty-six of forty-two built there as barter
elmina grandest patroness of them all
wings of floors reconstructed into such grandeur:
"the women's quarters have a most unpleasant, most befoul'd odor"
and thus the viewing balconies up above the sweltering human hum.

fort and forteress

but never you mind about that
for there's enough to go around and then—
300 miles of coast
60 known castles
remains of half as many
undisturbed
monuments to green and gold and silver god

cape coast built by hardy swedes 16 & 53
fort osu 16 & 61 by the very captives who would stand and die there
rotting blood into the
hard packed earth.

lust for gold
lust for blackest black of gold.
all so much whoring in the veins of a continent laid to waste
trading all along the coast
capturing and herding deep inside the hot interior
"oh, there be wealth enough for plenty,
and kingdom come before we bleeds 'em dry."

"decreed: that greater benin will export no more men as chattels; for to continue in that way should only weaken the core of our kingdom."
women and children remain free, however,
to be enslaved at any time.

and kingdom come indeed.

see also
senegambia
liberia
kingdom of kongo
sierra leone
gold coast
ivory coast
bight of biafra
bight of benin
southeast of africa from good hope to delgado and all of madagascar

why is it called cape of good hope?

sugar cotton coffee metals tobacco
shipping   finance   insurance
industry
such cities as amsterdam, liverpool, bristol
stade-en-lande whitehaven la rochelle and boston
rotterdam newport nantes lisbon
such kingdoms as _____ *(fill in the blank)*
and along north africa herself   indian ocean
and so-called middle east
sahara of shifting footprints

why is it called, do *you* believe, cape of *good* hope?

and then   of course   that red red red red sea

worlds   continents of exclusion
la trahison des clercs
the disironic unwillingness
of colonial powers to self-destruct—

mercantable movable property
chattel
res—
tyrannies of words thrown ad lib against the abject body—

there is no history of this world that is not written in black.

"The peoples of Europe, having exterminated the peoples of America, have been obliged to enslave the peoples of Africa and use them to clear all these lands for cultivation. Sugar would cost too much if the plant that produces it were not tended by slaves."
—from "Le droit de rendre les nègres esclaves"
De l'Esprit des lois
Montesquieu

seats of exchange
the counting houses
wealth of the new world:
raw materials   commodities produced
caravel
caravel
a word that floats along the tongue.

sugar rice molasses rum indigo spices cotton
continuing raids
forced marches
slaves and ivory
slaves and gold
raw materials   back and forth
back and forth
caravel
a word a world that floats upon the tongue.

sugar molasses indigo rice spices cotton rum
sugar cotton coffee metals tobacco
indigo rum   molasses
rice spices cotton

why does the industrial revolution occur simultaneously with the trade in black flesh?

"i hear someone saying—
hunh
the chain
the gang—oh-o-oh
. . . sound of the . . .
i'm'a leave that alone now"
—"Chain Gang" by Sam Cooke

nor does it matter what order we tell it.
only that we know it
once and for every all
know it as we know
our own breathing in the night

sugar cotton coffee metals tobacco
sugar cotton coffee metals tobacco
indigo rum   molasses
rice spices cotton
wealth of the new world
       and old king cotton
       his heart was so rotten
       they laid him out to die
       and here he comes again masquerading as "... the fabric of our lives"

"one day / we'll all be free."

there is a kind of churning in the gut that comes with the learning of history.
memory of old sea-sicknesses-unto-death?
a taste of bones ground up to make white bread?
ground up to make
refined white sugar?
polished into
pearl-white rice?
aged twelve years
into light smooth rum?
for the world
the wide wide world is fat
greased on bones from deep in the sea
oh but let us not speak yet of seas
let us never speak of seas
let us look instead across horizons to
other sides of these worlds we know
in the texts of our skins

colón and colonie
exercises in linguistic dexterity
west indies
east indies
french indies
dutch indies
and such
companies:

american islands company
royal african company
french senegal company
santo domingo company
guiana company
second louisiana company
new cayenne company
new france
and that much more
company
so very much
company
how long until application of the etiquette
that a great value of being good company
is knowing when to depart?

code noir   code noir   code noir

noted,
record of a crossing
1625:
five portuguese ships
bearing one thousand two hundred eleven african cargo
of which five hundred eighty-three die in transit
sixty-eight more within the first week of arrival at brazil.

"a little coffee to wake me
a bit of tea to comfort
sugar to sweeten
a taste of rum to cure me
a taste of rum all around
all around
all around
o a good swig o' rum all around"

status report:
1730 till 1780
glory days of the trade on american continent;
1746 till 1774 mortality rate aboard slave ships from nantes harbor
as much as thirty-four per cent.
1754 three hundred thousand enslaved in french west indies alone.
in 1780 numbers rise to six hundred seventy-three thousand there.
1786 good king louis orders improved work conditions:
>no "hard labor" sunset to sunrise—
>first mandate also
>of french two-hour lunch break.

a little leisure
a *little* leisure is a very good thing.
very little leisure so much the better.

status update:
1850 official end of the trade to brazil.
three million six hundred thousand imported later that year.

"so that MAN has indeed become
the coin of Africa. . . . ."

>sing:
>*Sugar for my coffee.*
>*Sugar for my tea.*
>*Posies at my footsteps.*
>*Don't you fancy me?*

and when you've finished singing

then bring me the tongue of any who use the word *slave* as metaphor for servitude
metaphor for addiction
as metaphor for love
metaphor for any thing
bring me their tongues
to tack up on the walls of those castles—
o fort and forteress—
by the saddest of the old old seas.
but do not let me speak.
bring me their tongues
no do not let *me* speak at all:

my curse is not even ripened yet.
and my mouth already is filled to the teeth with it.

only more such exercises in linguistic dexterity, in flow
the spanish crown proposes

the french crown proposes
the right christian portuguese king proposes
fra bartolomeo considers
fray bartolome de albornoz dissents

legerdemain by word of mouth
jests of tongue and teeth and palate:

emissary of the crown
explorer
sovereign and sovereignty
requerimiento
encomienda
african slave trade
internecine african warfare
development of 17th century *slaving states*
kidnapping, capture, hunting.
indenture, engagement, servitude.
tawny indian and blackamoor african
o call a spade a spade and get it over with—
human beings endowed with souls and requiring moral care and instruction?
devils in league with some master devil host?
call a slave a slave and be done with it

for *we* never are.
and *it* is never done.
series of ages-old adaptations and adjustments
improvisations and re-orderings
known universes
and concepts of kin
and all night gig rehearsals within the haunted texts of our haunted skin.
"you ain't seen nothing yet."

*"I left my hat / ba-doum-**doum** / in Haiti!"*

i'll just bet you did
o i'll just bet
"just a handful of gimme and a mouthload of much-obliged."

.

i want to know
i want to know
just tell me where to rest my malediction
for i cannot rest
i cannot rest until i smell that smell of blood
i cannot rest until i have again the sense
that i was born with
that something's rotten
every time i don my garments of yellow cotton
or see the slim black fingers of boys who play piano
or taste the first sip of dark dark rum
or sweeten my coffee
or tread the slave-bricked streets of my own city—
the wastes of downtown streets where
children
sell themselves for fast-food meals of ground meat and grease
and everything is everything
and nowhere is there satisfaction to be had
and the whole of history seems designed to render me sad
disconsolate
broken-hearted
and plain-old down.

aww
itchee-gitchee
gimme-gimme
acca-bacca
shaka-laka
down
down
down by the
riverside

O
"sound of the chain
the gang"
O
bye-bye blackbird-O

but for now
let us close our texts and rest our heads down on our arms.
it's best we take a rest: our lesson for the day is done.
and too
we must call ourselves ready next time we hear the knelling of the old school bell
ready ourselves for the next day's new season in hell

but for now we may well consider ourselves done
having come to the end of the addenda
to the preface for this introduction
of our little history
part one.

Canne à Sucre: A Slave-Song Suite

for J. B. Borders IV

your lips against me in the dark
expanse of face and shoulders
feel of back and breastbone
nothing but what they
are
how when you look
then history makes sense
comfort   consolation
the many uses of the body
words such as flesh meat undulation unguent funk
desire claim urgent flesh consume motion flesh

to live in desire
to live one's own desire—
and neither consolation nor despair—
to smell and taste how we cleave together and apart
my hand inside your middle
history there—
fruit left on a sill deep into summer—
my grandmother's clean cool and perfect hands on my cheeks
and i held between her knees looking up
brown hands folded across her skirted lap
her own so cool and perfect hands—
roof-tile slate grey eyes
full of memory and of longing—
i long for you now—
your face across generations
desire

akin to gluttony
bitter brown of cane
and warm inside
as the moment rum
explodes its silence in the waiting mouth
—a wish?—
aguardiente the slave-men say
aguardiente
agua como amor
su amor como agua, mi señor, slave-women respond—
in full view
brick walls old as cities old in time
brick walls older than the many deaths breathed into them so—
agua y tierra, mi señor
agua y tierra y sangre, papí
agua   ardiente   como   amor—
i see you through my grandmother's eyes
roof-slate grey
i feel her hands in yours
the love she bore down into ash:
he consoled me, she said for no reason one day
consoled me.
and the twins were born.

often in the middle of an afternoon
a train calls
hooting its way to present tense

your dark hand on my thigh
consoling
driving
invoking
a kind of collapse we come to long for once we've known
comes unasked
resisted   ill-defined
shuddering from somewhere underneath
the bowels
and fear of biblical proportion
and then we bear
into

the heft of centuries
blood and sugar borne living from some field outside the city
sugar that burns
into teeth and lips and gums
consolation
the nearness of our slave-i-tude—
inside the city
free-women in tignons and turbans
leaf sandals wrapping their feet
copper and gold ringing ankles and wrists
brown and naked beneath single-layered dresses
"made for loving" the old ones cluck and watch them go
"born for it" the only known response—
sting of sugar and of blood lacing the milk they pass into the warm mouths of
their own infants
their men—
and fingers and lips that circle and smile
and the dreaming that does not shy away
but sucks and sucks until the cane is soft
soft as bagasse—
"you sweetness you" the old say to the young
ma canne à sucr'

i turn to you in bed centuries
of made-for-loving hammering in my head and thighs
canne à sucre i mouth into your mouth
bed of moss
brick walls and floors
your hands like coffee
roasted
ready to serve up
sweetness
(ah, ma douceur)
lips of a woman
or small child
eternal kiss from where the cane grows straight tall pliant beyond dreams

back breastbone and hands and lips

consume

consume

consume away

the burning building up the dying again
born to it
borne
as warriors are born—

brown babies carrying history like sacks of yam to market—
born to consume away
to die   resurrect
claim   motion   urgent   meat   desire
claim undulation claim consume
claim flesh
to cleave
and cleave
together and apart
and warm inside—
how when you look they are nothing but what you
live

in
against in all

the dark
and bitter brown of
cane.

5.

unfinished coffees

Everything Happens to (Monk and) Me

for J. B. Borders IV

we hustle hard as the rest of the folk me and my baby
but it never seems to count.
so
we stop off nights and hear the best and worst of everybody.
my baby's down in heart but that hasn't stopped him yet.
me i'm just down.
we struggle-in.
we sit ourselves down.
we believe in everything.
we know the other life is a club called havana.
we dream in unison how it will be there
and have never had this conversation because we do not need to.
we believe in everything my baby and me.
we *know* that life on the other side is a club called havana
and sometimes we ache for it
but not out loud.

the music in this city is not heard in clubs.
this is not a thing we recite
we know this
by heart.
no.
it's in the thrumming of the empty streetcar tracks
the thrumming of the old wooden banqettes beneath the newer cement
it's in the bricks the slaves are cursing over eternally
the way the poorest of the crazies look up from rheumy eyes
the way a workingman hauls his haunches home to his woman
a little low on one side his walk
a little bit too hurried or too slow
for him for her one
the way she doesn't wait but puts his plate over water

pretending to watch the news
washing her hands
or else not stirring
pretending not to daydream
over porkchops and brown gravy

the thrumming is in the way it hangs
the whole city hanging
at the edge of a water no one will wade
the whole city hanging
the way the not-so-young-anymore men used to say
"can you *hang* with that?" and mean it
mean it.
that's the problem with this city
we *all* mean it so hard.
and this is a soft city
a city of softness
turning turning ever on the edge of its own meaning
and hanging on to *us* for dear life.
we really
really
mean
to get it right soon some glorious day some soft thrumming night
and "oh" cry out the pretty little street-stepping-boys sometimes
"ain't we righteous, y'all!"
yes sweetness we mouth in their direction when we hear or see or care
we really truly are

and that's what started the whole damn thing to begin with:

me and my baby just want to hear some music from time to time.
well i do.
my baby he loves me and sometimes just says okay.
and sometimes he just fakes it like he doesn't have this longing.
my baby thinks he's stoic—
that old negro stoicism sterling loved so.
but no
he wouldn't be so sad around the eyes late evening into night
after supper and before cigarettes
—we still have supper here
and late-night breakfast
and say "good evening" after twelve noon—
he wouldn't have those *eyes*
not from being old-fashioned sterling/negro-stoic
oh-but-no we say here (first syllable stressing)
truth is he's old-fashioned negro-martyr heroic.
i get him.
then i get him out.
we get out into or behind the crowd
we do not need to look at one another
we nod
we hang our hands about as if we've known it all along.
we thrum
we thrum
we thrum
inside the city

at least that's how it is
when we condescend to our hipper selves

"oh baby" we say together later on
"oh
oh, baby"

but ain't we righteous y'all?

and out of nowhere in the night
solo
standards
the funny-sad
the halved
the tired
witty
unlovely chords
and everything within us that ever hoped for hipness stirs.
not following that sound
we laugh into the night
because we were young once
and very very hip.
we were young once
and very very wise.
we were young once
these streets were always ours
we paved them with the flats of our heels
we danced
and never bothered to tire
or if we did it hardly mattered
our hippest coolest livest selves
out late and full up with heart
valiant as the very streets
we wind we wind me and my baby
we reach the other side the place called havana
we reach our own unlovely selves
—bitter chords—
reach for each other
and are wise
enough to know better
our tender places older than before.

it never ends.
we follow the sweep of the river downtown and up.
somewhere is music we can hear
havana and unlovely chords
and right here with us
the city and the indigo night
its tuneless keyboard silent altogether for the moment
we play upon the night
each key a treasure we have close-*tight* between us
unrighteous
and unlovely
full up with longing
in the streets.

Expeditus

"you say you believe
we are all the same in the end.
this is what you want to believe
now that you have your freedom.
let me tell you, wise man
i was born with this freedom and i do not trust the white man
        to pass me in the square without cutting me down.
        or his woman in her house there in the town
        to send him to cut me for a lark.
and i was born with the freedom
given you these last few days.
but because you are a christian
let me give you an example
so that you do not think hard of me.
here is an example.
you yourself are a christian.
you call yourself a christian and a catholic.
well so do i.
but with me it is a point of law.
freeborn as i am
i do not break the law when i can help it.
that as you can see is just good sense.
since i myself am a man of the law.
but let me show you.
st. expeditus.

you know the story.
they will not admit its truth
but everyone has heard the story by now.
a roman soldier.
a figure from a crowd,
a group scene intended for the foot of a crucifix.
a simple roman soldier.
not a warrior of distinction.
not a charioteer. no.
a foot soldier.
a member of a motley
and anonymous assembly.
and they lift him up.
they give him the status of sainthood.
and the laws on their books say we must carry out
       every crisis
       every moment of import in our lives
       under the offices of this holy catholic church.

"we are all the same you say.
and here they have us
       fools and cowards that we are, one,
       bending and praying
       to a painted plastered foot soldier.
we are all the same in the end, you say.
all the same.

"here is a figure i draw in the dirt.
a secular figure, clearly.
will you pray to it?
no. no. now you will not pray.
but you will go and kneel in the dust at the doors of their churches
and you will pray to a poor foot soldier
who never intended to be separated
from the rest of his kind.
you think your freedom buys you this.
and this
and this and this.
and i tell you i can not walk across that square
without knowing i can be cut down in a moment's passing.
or you—
your catechism
your rosary pressed to your bosom.
do you think this is why they got you your freedom
—the brothers of the lodge—
to make you free to kneel on dirt or stone floors at the backs of churches
to see them swing the censers
to hear about the purgatory
set aside
for just such as your color and my own?
well.
enough of this.
here are papers to be made over.
what was your trade in bondage?
what did you do?"

"iron.
i worked in iron.
i helped to build the iron that holds the great houses secure.
i helped to build the gates the doors the windows and their bars.
throughout this whole city you can see my labor—
walls and gates and doors and windows
wrought of iron
and tempered all in vèvès.
i helped to make the curse
that cures this wretched city
that sends it year after year
into the great god's sea.

"you are freeborn, avocat.
       freeborn. and thus you think you must
       teach and reform a poor slave brother.
yes i stand and kneel outside their churches.
yes i cover my head in crosses and choke on dust.
i pray to expedite
because i know the labor of waiting
of biding time.
do i care if he is false or true?
do i care if he is given me in ignorance or else to throw me into confusion?
you say he is but a foot soldier.
well i have been a slave
a slave and a foot soldier too.
you think i have not been on forced marches to

their spanish colonies to the east?
or that i do not know that you too were made to go?
you think i have not served to guard this walled city
roused out of sleep or loving or dreaming i was loving
there in the quarters behind the great house?
when you have been a slave
what is the indignity of a foot soldier?

"i tell you that i have prayed to expeditus.
speed o speed o fast deliver me
here are chains that bind me
here are stones that weight me
succor
mercy
and a quick deliverance

yes.
i have prayed these very words, avocat.
and i will live to see you pray them
as you cut across the square."

The Evening News: *A Letter to Nina Simone*

a wail
a whoop
a line brought back from nowhere.
deep violet of memory,
stored up against hard times' coming.
we were righteous then,
experienced in things we had not seen
but always knew
would pass this way.

we had righteousness on our side.

they say you stood before a small audience in
    new orleans last year and abused them for their smallness.
not just their numbers
but their looks.
their soulless way of sitting
and waiting to be entertained.
they told me how you stood there and cursed them good.
told me how they took it
for the sake
of all they used to be so long ago they never could forget.
could only say like the old folk, when cornered perhaps,
said *"i disremember"*

i asked them what you wore.

i remembered the years i struggled with the very private fear
that i would remain a child forever
and miss all that was major in our one moment of glory.
even a child knows there is one such moment.
one.
even i had sense enough to see you and not weep.
even a child then understood the words
"sister"
"brother"
"people"
"power"

and anyone could see we were all the evening news.

and hear you sing—
at least that was what they called it.
it was my best girlfriend's sister
who came up on us closed off in her bedroom
laughing over her cosmetics, her jewelry, her sex, her t.v.
and instead of sending us out
leaned there in the doorway and smiled.
"you two know so much,
want to be so grown and everything,
need to quit all that giggling
and learn to listen to nina."
that was late autumn.
aletha came into her own bedroom and sat between us on the bed.
she turned up the volume
but did not change the station.
we watched her and her college friends
in dashikis and afros
on the evening news.

that year marceline and i listened close
to the lyrics and the ways
the easy breaths and breathless lines
the underground silences
of you and roberta.
we argued and sassed,
slapped hands on our hips at the slightest provocation,
and learned when and when not to apologize for it.
two brown girls acting out,
mothers looking out over our heads that way they had then
whenever we went so far we did not need to be told.
we gave our telephone numbers to those boys
with the hippest walks
the better grade of afro
the deep-changing voices,
and we never took their calls.
we danced the sophisticated sissy
the thing
the shake
the go-on
the soul strut.
we counted our girlfriends
"soul sister number 1"
"soul sister number 2."
marceline learned to cornrow
and i braided my older brother's bush each night.
we were too much and we knew it.
we thought we understood it all.

deep violet
deep violet

but that was years ago.
and you were in your glory then.

then,
while i was still younger than i knew or admitted,
and studying in the south of france,
i danced four nights out of five and all weekend,
my arms on the hips or shoulders
of some wiry brother from cameroun or ivory coast
senegal, algeria, panama, martinique,
one of only six or seven young black women at university
among the dozens and dozens of dark men who circled us
weaving their weightless cloth
their heavy guard.
escorted when i would have been alone
fed when i had no hunger
driven when i lacked a destination
protected from the mere possibility of danger—
and danger to them
we knew
meant "frenchmen/
whitemen"—
courted and cossetted
and danced into sleeplessness.
"you will be old one day, sister.
then, you will sleep fine."
but their hearts,
the dark wiry hearts of the brothers,
were in the right places.

the foolish ones said
"you are like women of my country"
and feigned weaknesses no one would believe
they ever even remotely had known.
and often enough
had the immediate good sense
to laugh at themselves
and then at the rest of us.
the others did something like waiting,

danced endlessly, and at the end of evening said
"i have this sister,
this nina.
play some for my sister here, man.
man, get up and put on that nina simone."
and we sat in the silence in the dark
as one found the shiny vinyl
and put the needle to the darker groove.
we sat choked with roman cigarettes
too much dancing
too much good food.
we sat listening and did not touch.
we looked at one another's hands
and read recognition there.
one day we would be old.
we would sleep
and no longer know one another.
we sat into the night
until we grew hungry again and sick from the stale air.
we listened
we wailed
we did not touch
or bow down our heads.

and that is the meaning
of the word *expatriate.*

if you live right
if you live right
if you live right

but what has living done for you?

i heard your voice
over the radio late one night in cambridge
telling how you never meant to sing.
whoever interviewed you hardly said a word.
he asked his questions
and you took your time.
you breathed long breaths between phrases,
your speaking voice lighter
and less lived in than i remembered.
you sang a line or two
and talked about your "life."
i asked my question
directly into the speaker—
"what the hell did living do for you, girl?"
i sat on the floor and drank my coffee.
i paced the carpet between your pauses.
i pulled my nightdress up in both hands and danced.
but i got no satisfaction that night.
and, for what it matters,
heaven did not come to me either.

don't talk to me about soul.
don't tell me about no damned soul.
years and years and years
of *all night long*
and-a where are you
and making time and doing right.
expatriate years.
years, woman, years.
where *were* you?

and then you sang "Fodder on My Wings"
with not a note of holy in your voice,
and what could i do?
a young woman,
i put myself to bed.

it was the following year
that you cursed them down in new orleans.
dragged for them like muddy water.
i listened to the story on the telephone
or looked into the faces i came on in the streets.
"what"
i asked them
"did she wear?"
and do you think they could tell me?
all i asked the people
was *what did the woman have on?*

and what about it?
if your country's full of lies
if your man leaves you
if your lover dies
if you lose your ground and there is no higher ground
if your people leave you
if you *got* no people
if your pride is hurting
if you got no pride, no soul
if you living in danger
if you living in mississippi, baltimore, detroit
if you walk right, talk right, pray right
if you don't bow down
if you hungry
if you old
if you just don't know
please
please
outside-a you there is no /
place to / go
these are the expatriate years, these.
what is left.

the people dragged their sorry asses out to see you
and you cursed them
you looked out into their faces, those you could see
and accused them
you called them down for all those years.
you sang the songs you sand when you were younger

and you made them pay.

and then
deep violet
and a longer time no one will speak of.

dear nina,
i want to say to you how we did not mean it.
how we did not mean to give you up
to let you go off alone that way.
i want to say how we were a younger people, all of us.
but none of it is true.
we used you
and we tossed what we could not use to the whites
and they were glad to get it.
we tossed you out into such danger
and closed our eyes and ears to what was to become of you
in those years—
deep
deep violet—
and worst of all
we did not even say your name.
we ate you like good hot bread
fresh from the table of an older woman
and then we tossed the rest out for the scavengers.
does it matter?

does it matter when and how we did it to you?
does it matter we got no righteousness from it?
that we felt no shame?
does it matter we took all good things in excess then,
and then again?
not only you
but all things?
does it matter we sometimes return to you now,
in the back rooms of childhood friends,
forgiven lovers?
does it matter this is no gift or tribute or right or holy thing
but just a kind of telling
a chronicle to play back
against those images that never quite made it
to the evening news?

how cursed,
how sorry a mess of people can we be, nina
when outside-a you
there is no place
to go?

Litany of Our Lady

our lady of the sidewalks
the pavements and the crumbling brick
the mortar rock and oyster-shell roads
our lady of sorrows and sadnesses
of intolerable agonies tolerated daily
of drifters grifters scrappers and scrapers
our lady of dudes and dicks and pricks
of petty thieves and of whoremongers
of piss-swelled gutters
and dives
and the grimed-over windows knotty-haired children peer through;
our lady
our lady of boys shot down in the dark
dying in open lots along lesser used roads leading out of town
of old men beneath interstates
       sitting, standing, walking a block or so away and back;
our lady of lost and found and forgotten
cast-off ditched
of what was and never will be again
of aggrieved and bereft
accused indicted surrendered up to death
of old tar-colored women in plain or checkered housedresses
      telling aloud their rosaries and rosaries
        and rosaries of faith;
our lady of ladies
and of church-ladies-in-waiting
of young girls with hard uncertain breasts
      and promises of school and school
        and more school even than that;

our lady of go-cups and fictionary tours
cigar bars absinthe bars
of coffee houses open all night and churches closed all day
              for-admittance-please-ring-bell-and-wait
and wait;
our lady of antiques dealers dealing in saints
              in crosses, weeping cemetery angels, prayer cards
              in praline mammies, cigar shoppe indians
              in dwarf nigger jockeys whose heads have been lopped off
                         and stand
                         one hand outstretched, one cocked at the hip
                         seeming not to be waiting but bargaining dealing
                              for the return of their heads
      their heads their perfectly round perfectly lovely little nappy nappy heads;

our lady
our lady of tired buildings listing to one side
and brick-between-cypress posts that simply will stand
as houses themselves give way around falling-down stairs
leaving only a something
a memory of a structure
of spanish-tiled roofs and batten shutters
in a swamp
of a city
of ironworks and of plaster
o, lady lady
our lady of anything
at all

✝

Suicide City

i turn in bed toward my lover
how his skin
hugs to the bony parts
nothing in excess
and nothing missing.
my lover's eyes are closed.
my lover's eyes are often closed.
he cannot see
the fine trophy i make of his fine hide
the smell of him clinging
and the forbidden thing
the forbidden thing between us like a weight.

night and day and night still following upon night
the coming of spring is a difficult thing.
we here in the city
mornings stand about a lumpen horde
all our smells commingled with the city air
with dust and traffic
cheap greasy breakfasts transported in bags by working-men—
faces altogether lacking in sleep—
smelling as they do of hard soap and unfinished coffees
school-children with their knapsacks loaded down with nothing
              of value
we stand about the busstops and press against each other
              when it comes
we are grateful for a seat and turn our heads to windows or to books
to newspapers or one another
we are grateful to have such destinations
obligations that remove us
from ourselves
we nod and tip good-mornings
we hum inside the humming streetcar
we hum inside our humming bodies
and all our secrets safe at least for now.

night in the city is a maddening deafening
opening
of hot blossoms
azalea
jasmine
cereus
great roses brought by europeans long ago
sweet olive pouring over weekend stench
we pour ourselves into the city streets
or lock ourselves behind our doors
its doors
or else we turn and turn beneath plain sheets
and ceiling fans
our mouths our lovers' mouths
our hands their hands
we turn and turn
and do not look away

sex inside the city is almost communal.
the street creeps in
the children across the gate
the sirens and the shouts of drunks
the poor
the mad
the broken
the late
we cry out together
in time to hear their cries.
we look ahead to sweat and moans to come
collapse and seize ourselves each other
we do not whisper
cause we know no one cares:
their lovers all are boarding streetcars at the track.

long long long the night it has no end.

we moan and turn and call on names we had forgotten.
we pull ourselves up by our feet.
we drink night-water
taste our mouths that taste of spit and kisses
urinate longer than we care to
scratch our behinds
look out windows
meander back to bed
we sleep there.
or hump.
or say "are you alright" for absolutely no reason.
we do not listen to the outside.
we know that it lurks.
it listens.
it knows our names.

the forbidden thing between us like a weight
it waits until we sleep
and then
the city all around us and we dream
all together in our tribe we dream the city back to sleep
we shield our fears
lovers
turning
ever turning in the night
the city dreams us back alive
and all our dreams forbidden
thrumming
eternal
at the track.

meditation is an urban preoccupation.
country people poke fun, they laugh.
here in the city
we all go mad together and simply refuse to tell.
we are so superior
we meditate
we spout the latest world report
we lock church doors
pay tax on candles and prayer cards
sing under our breaths walking the bright streets at night
we practice breathing last breaths
—but we have not forgotten how to sing—
we open our mouths and are wise
nights we go home to one another
fearful of the sounds
the smells of spring
a difficult thing to deny
our confidence
a thing left at the door
a useful thing sure
but home is home after all
and there we are alone and naked for all the city to see.
hurry
hurry we want to warn one another
it comes
it dreams
it knows our names.

the city looked up one day and was free.
not from yellow fever or flood or torrents of affliction
not whoring or debt or the stench of standing waters
not from cults of destitution
the union roosting, its naive bravado
coteries of saviors bearing bibles in arms:
all in that way abiding.
it happened that way didn't it?
was that the way it was?
whole city of slaves
name of jude eulalie andré amalie josefína adelína ambrose martinet
ariane flavio zuma placide adão obade mattoso teresinha jérémie
mathieu hilaire robért roseangela marcus albertine nicolette cúde
jean-lùc louis luís théard théophile ti-nom ti-bert ti-jean ti-ton
down from kongo senegambe são tomé nzadi ngola san domingue
over waters of the dead:
large river river nzadi river kongo
river atlantic
to mesachabe
big muddy-big-water all over again.
and so the city looked up that one day and was free
free from the indigo the brick factory
the cane fields the rice fields
but oh the bordellos the church the households
the ward heelers the back rooms the dirty linen
the cigar factories the baker shops
the little merchants and their small merchandise
cigar-rollers shoemakers praline-women sawyers wainwrights
the lavatrice the coachman the drayman the cook
the builder
the builder

but oh the city looks back and says its own name and who answers?
who hears?
not drums alone
but also the bare foot against red brick
against italian marble sometimes or tile
the blue-brown-violet throats of bad or good children
of old men keening
harpish voices of women too young to be so old
the closing of a rheumy cataracted eye
the swallow of bloodied throat late into the knife-fight no one wins
the evergoing thrumming of the night
the hard summer days
the sounds of leaves about to fall
sound of a papa's voice from his tomb
the doors that scrape and close and hesitate to scrape and close
sound of that river turning on its belly our belly
the near-words of the near-dead

again
in this city
in *this* city
everything comes again
where we take nothing to the streets
it waits for us there and is it any wonder
is it any wonder
we wander through the slick the dark the foul-sweet streets
in all this darkest black of night
where some round-headed boy
centuries younger than he knows
claps hands to keyboard or to horn
to microphone or congo-cheek
and says so softly
someone gave this song to me?

every night
every single night
it happens in exactly this way
inside this city
that someone's child should say that thing
that we would go to hear and see him say it
would tell him
play oh play that thing
that horn that key that drum that throat that thing you play
*just **play** it baby*
and all our secrets safe
at least for now?

we go home.
we go home turn keys in doors and laugh and do not forget.
in this city nothing has been forgotten.
that one great sin we cannot claim.
it knows
it waits
it comes again
we see it in the eyes we come on in the street
we see it in the eyes of lovers turning away or toward us
we see it in the braces of the streetcar tracks
we hear it taste it feel it breathe it in each day
every day
we are so wise
we go home
we are so hip
we go home
we are so faithful in our turning
it comes on us unawares
and then we sweat.

oh but the city is not fooled.
it knows it is the lover who is not blind but merely sleeps.
it knows we know it is the dreamer
turning huge back
away from us to hump
toward us to dream
to dream us back alive each night
so that we wake
thrumming
eternal
ever
at the tracks.

6.

what hunger

Desire and Private Griefs

I.
the kind of man you would call on
to carry your dead mother up on his shoulders
a genuine furrow lining his brow
setting down her remains
with the grace of one who had expected to be called
at just such a time
and so had become prepared to do his duty
by the living
the dead
had not turned his back on your grieving
but stood somewhat apart
some respectful distance
between the sight of your huge grief
and the guilty love you had come to put to rest.

i named him that first time
—sterling, son—
some dead uncle's name.
even then i could see he knew
the turning away that comes to even the bravest.
and then there was the challenge of this hunger
writing the years
across my body.

it was a dangerous affair from the start.

2.

the first thing you learn about desire
is that it does not wear down with time.
there comes a time when you can no longer get your pleasure
but the desire stays with you—
a dampish kind of feeling
beneath the armpits
at the back of the tongue

i stand across a banquet hall from him
a desk
a room
the gravesite of someone i cared too little for in life.
he will not look into my face.
(the damp.
the quiet.)
i take him home
accustomed to the kinds of rumors generated
at times like this.
(he has that weary look he wears so beautifully
and tracks graveyard dust
onto my freshly cleaned floors.)
i do not touch him until he is naked
his head cradled lightly
in the damp bend of my lap.

it is all so familiar—
the cleaving
the hunger
the years do not relieve.

years pass.
one day no reply will come at all.
(an aunt or someone who knew us both
will send the news.
it will do no good trying to get home in time.
they will have laid him aside
weeks before i can have known.
a newspaper clipping
a photograph from years ago.)
how can it have gone on so long?
he means his own longevity
my returning ever so often only to find
ruined cities i must go to immediately
the meetings on the floors of jazz clubs and cultural caucus affairs
the grey hairs heaped upon his head
his heart greying against me
the inability to give or get satisfaction
in spite of all the rubbing in the dark.
he will not ask for mercy
and i make no offers, no kind gestures.

it was a dangerous affair from the beginning he says to me.
he looks at me across a tiny, papered table.
i do not hear the claims he makes.
i know better.
and i do not pretend to be a kind woman.

later
he goes with me to the airport.
i'm too old for this his smile wants to say.
been too old for this a long time now.
the first thing you learn about desire i almost answer
it will eat you alive. if you let it.
he puts a cigarette to his mouth as if to ask *how long?*
i step out from the yellow checker cab
—years pass—
i too begin to bury my dead
begin to grey along the edges.
nothing ends.

3.
cairo
madrid
aix-les-bains
brazil
antigua
i send him cards
letters.
wherever i go
i sit down to write.
sometimes he replies
not often
but well.
we understand one another
—finally—
and it has taken so long.

he sends photographs
his head gone completely white
a brief smile
his letters do not mention
the names of the dead he continues to bury—
relatives
friends
the relatives of childhood playmates.

he talks to me of aging
if i were younger one letter begins.
my own letters
often are no more than travelogues
landscapes at best.
his are maps of time
bottled and stoppered
—if less than airtight—
and carry the motley smells
of home.

i send him gifts—
my fingernails
twists of hair form the nape of my neck
scarves i find in trinidad and algiers.

4.
death changes some things:
the way you feel about your mother
the path you take to get to a cousin's house
the greetings you give out
at casual meetings and such
the kind of woman you call on
to stand for your dead
—a genuine sorrow drawn across her face—
you trust her to grieve for you
without interfering in your fate.

she will not speak of guilts and broken promises
the losses she has suffered
written plainly beneath her eyes.
she lends an air of grace to the procession
the only woman not wearing black—
a tan or charcoal grey dress
altogether lacking in severity
hat cocked to one side
feathers and jewels—
she looks across the gravesite
a certain blankness to her stare.
she turns only after the others have done so—
a private grief that does not surface.

she leaves alone
carrying the heavy silences
of the dead.

House of the Dead Remembering (*House of Mercies / Variation 2*)

this bone-sack you see
held together with twine worn almost smooth
once danced and shook the bamboula.
now it makes one piece
with the blues you bring me
served up like sunday dinner
the borrowed sound
of your borrowed hurt
neatly arranged by the same brown fingers
that touch my face
and tend the plants out back.
and the days like an old man in soft-soled shoes
picking up his walk
from the backs of his thighs
remembering to catch up his pants knees
before squatting to sit
in the company of women.

this chamy bag holds together the past
of the house where i was born
house of mercies
made of dry rot and tenpenny nails
house of mercies
holding up the sky
keeping it from falling
into the swampy earth
house of mercies
where my mother ate the dry bread of silence
where my grandfather managed

to stride through death unaided
upright
through the front-room window
of the house he built
where my grandmother insisted
that as children we learn
the many proper ways
to honor our dead
because memory is everything.

and what is it you bring me
carried in your arms
like a still-born child you insist on naming?
nothing more than your own bruised past
rolled between the fingers of your good left hand
and treated like trouble
because you want more from me
than this fallow language
would have you say.
why can't you see
how we are both just borrowed against time
like so much grieving
saved up in the corners of a house
that recognizes no past
and everyone goes on living
only to honor the dead
to eat this dry crust
without relish
or desire?

your youth is gone.
my youth is leaving me.
you want what i want:
some guarantee against forgetfulness
in the way we go about our lives
some proof that death is something more
than throwing dirt in the face
and turning to walk away
some hope against the awesome forgetting
when we go into the ground.

when we were younger
and i moved against you in the bed mamma left me
your eyes part closed
your mouth open
breathing loud
do you remember what you used to say?
loose me, loose me
i held you even closer
dragging you quicker and deeper
into the smell of our locked bodies
my bones
your bones
my body that carried no children to remember us by
loose me you begged me
but i never set you free.
memory is everything.

you sit in the room
you outfitted for yourself.
i sit at my desk
facing out on the slave-bricked street below.
we want to believe
in the both of our lives
of passion and much grieving.
we want some proper antidote
to the pasts we have accumulated
living as we have
in this house of death and remembering
the dry crusts of our younger selves
like so many photographs
scattered among the objects
that measure out our years

the architecture of two lovers
growing old
in a wood-frame house
and nothing more.

Evidence of Conjure

. . . and you
your face that perfect brown
your eyes and their darker places inked all around
your hands that touched mine
—so casual a thing—
as if you could not touch some other way
full of "friendship"
mercy
and the other thing.

your eyes and hands, the soft shock of your mouth
damp and curved like a woman's or a boy's.
we talked of things that mattered
and when we'd run through those of those that did not.
you leaned. i sprawled onto you there—
the front window up
the candle for my dead blown out nearby.
you think you know
but i can look only at your eyes and see you don't and say:
had you been more careful
it should never have come to this—
the leaning and the sprawling
the way you sat or stood or lay
the covers pulled back behind you

the way you drew me to you in one motion or a dozen
your mouth inside outside around my mouth.
and when you kissed my belly and put your hands deep in me
you took the whole of my body into yours and did not give it back.

keep it.
i want to say how it was this way.
nor am i ashamed to tell you now:

i am saving all this to use against you later.

lover,
the wind is like a cousin at the door—
persistent
and having finally so little to tell.

i sit and listen for lack of any pressing thing to do.
and somewhere, home,
leagues and leagues away from where i am
your body
sleek and brown and very very comfortable in its skin
—nothing in excess
nothing wanting—
the tuft of hairs above beneath your lips
the smell of strong tobacco hugging to your palms
hands in your pockets—

none of this was planned.
none of it.
i close my eyes and throat and this is what is left:
your body rubbing mine
all its evidence of conjure laid bare
the dry insistent patience
of time and distance and other lives to live and to let go of
a lusting distant, palpable, ready to lay hold
at the first and merest sign
of weakening
of remembering
of open-faced desire.

the catch is this:
there is only one of you
about so tall
so broad
a certain shade of purest brown
—the solid stuff that any man is made of.
perhaps there is only one of me.
and that also
i am holding in evidence against you.
i am holding all i can manage
hoarding in my throat
my lips my tongue the slightest space between my teeth
between my legs along my breasts and spine
back of my head

every time you suck your breath up
or pull me to you in a sweat—
i am hoarding

every time you look in my direction or away

say my name or any other word in any other language

every curve your body cuts in time or any known or lesser known dimension

every touch you give to any other person or yourself

you seem not to understand
but i am using all of this
as evidence of the mojo worked against my body.

i should perhaps have said so early on
but this is conjure
—i know it when i see it taste it smell it—
and strange as it seems
it will last much longer
be that much harder to undo
the longer you wait.

and every time you close or open
your hands your eyes
your chamy bag
the hollow space at the very base of your head

—call it conjure hoodoo wanga mojo what you will—
but i am shoring saving hoarding it all in evidence against you.
i understand the uselessness of struggle. do you?
i come from this.
what's your excuse?

Freeing Your Hands

i sit cross-legged near the window
eating the last of the pears you brought me
and watch the spaces on the tree limbs
where the snow was.
i like to invent you in grey woolens
entering from a side-porch in charleston or memphis
(st. louis on bad days).
it wants to be spring.
the immediacy of your day shows in the way you approach
empty-handed
tired but valiant—
the way a man can only be
in charleston or memphis—
negro-gentleman-style
circa 1938.

instead you come toward me
out of place in this city
out of sorts at home
and smiling
the continuum of dissatisfaction
written like prophecies
in the creases above your eyes.
you come like a man who has read all the primary sources
trying hard to believe in the substance
of all he ought to believe.
you come like a man looking back—
almost heroic for a moment
(and the laughter like a hat you swore you'd never part with)—
you come carrying things
freeing your hands from being too beautiful.

and when i look into your face, what do i see?
the animal eyes you promised to save
for gazing into the hearth
of the kind of home
where a man could buttress himself
against even those pasts
faithful as the snows.

when my turn comes
i invent myself in black skirts.
a tan house in memphis
a walled courtyard in new orleans.
it can begin with a man
entering empty-handed
from a side-porch
inventing the moment where i stop inventing
where coffee-colored men everywhere put hands in trouser pockets
valiant,
tragic perhaps,
but always
looking back.

Movement I / part one

there is a movement in the dark that will not wait
the touch of fingertips and tongues
dry itch gone altogether damp
bones oiled and lengthened of their own motions;
take all you want the body seems to warn
you get but one such movement in the dark.

(again):

the night is no more for the brave
than passion for the sweet or pure of heart.
the night is littered with the frightened and the shamed.
the dark belongs to those of us who lust;
and lust to those who turn to face our fate and quiver.
there is a kind of dying becomes (the) daylight
the night belongs to us
who linger long
and seldom wait.

we all have been young and beautiful
or simply young and bold.
we all have seen our bodies stretched out beneath full sun
and felt such awe.
these selfsame bodies have so betrayed us so many times
and anyway perhaps no longer do the things they used to do.

perhaps we envy our own selves our younger selves.

perhaps we
are content to cloak these bodies in whatever cloaks them well.

perhaps we
turn and murmur turn and sigh.

perhaps we stay too long on the edges of our own small pasts
and wait out whatever dangers we find there.

or else it does not matter we are warned
forewarned
foresworn.

we look back once

or simply do not bother to stay—
what does it matter?

these bodies know
their own sad limitations better than we ever hoped to know or say.

and anyway
we get but one such movement in the dark.

i am here with you in the dark
i am
in this
deepest
blackest
darkest
so
with *you*
again.

do not murmur when i turn to face you
do not touch me
do not say that you have waited
wanting
do not lie
wait
forgive
deny
or ponder.
only lust.
fill up on it and full
taste gently softly fearsome
with just the slightest tip of tongue—
see how it has the taste of neither salt nor sweet?
animal funk soft enough to find your way by?
now is hardly time for taking or for giving mercy.
time now to strike or thirst and die.
time now to loose these lost or losing selves way past desire.
a something here—our own.
this simple urgent
shifting
in such dark.

Against the Bone

afternoons
i rubbed the length of your thigh and hip beneath the covers.
you pressed your face across the entire wide plain
between my breasts.
you spoke words into that space,
against the bone,
words i never fully heard
or cared to comprehend.
it was enough to feel your hands working their hoodoo
in and around
the hollow places between my meat and bone.

distance and the years and the dying:
these stand between us,
preventives to the kind of desire
that makes no allowance
for sobriety
or discretion.
there is danger still between us here,
tactile as a child's warm breath at prayer-time,
and remembrance like stones about our waists.
but this much i can tell:
how some mojo, once worked,
cannot be undone
not for love or money
guilty dreamings
or death—
and
long years from now
on sacred ground
we will have these stones between us
to count
and weigh
and rub together.

Memory No. 1

I.
i sit in the front parlor
the window open from the floor
the hard rain rushing in
stinging like fire-ants
against my feet
the little cloth navy pumps mamma had given me
set to one side
out of the wet.

do you know what hunger is?

i sit with the water
moving about my feet
remembering what it feels like to be touched:
my mother's hands parting my oiled hair
down the center
across the front;
my mother's hands bearing down on my back
rolling a little from place to place
as if
there were some secret place she could touch me
to help me cry
and just be done with it;
hands of some hoodoo woman
cradling my face
bathing me in bamba and sweet basil
feeling with her fine wet hands
along my skull
along my spine;
the hands of lovers who thought they knew
something of desire—
good men some of them
with no way of knowing
how their own hands would betray them;
you percy
down on your knees on the hardwood floor

arms wrapped about me
groping with your palms and fingers
along my hips
my thighs:
please woman please
that's what you said each time you bit my brown flesh
sucking up the little traces of blood
between clenched teeth.
did i cry?
did i cry?
no.
it was you kept saying
you got your hands on me woman
god-have-mercy you got your hands on me
but you stayed
didn't you?

you stayed the night.
you stayed all day the next day.
and when you came back the night after that
you said you wouldn't come again
you'd go home to your wife
do all a man could,
give me anything—
if i'd just take my hands off you.
i remembered your eyes, percy.
i don't know how to beg
that's how you said it
i don't know how to beg
but please
woman please
you got your hands on me and i just can't live like this

you walked out of the house
and across the porch.
you broke off a stem of geranium in the corner.
i saw you press it tight between your fingers.
they smell of iron i said to you then
always smelled of iron to me
like blood percy
like blood

i walked over to where you crouched above the flowering clay pots.
i put one hand into your near-kinky hair.
percy i said
percy
don't you know what hunger is?

The Wastrel-Woman Poem

she goes out in the night again
wastreling about
her thin-woman blues
slung over one shoulder
an empty satchel
one carries out of habit.

the first time you see her
you think her body
opens some new forbidden zone.
you think she has something to do with you.
she never does.
at least not the way you mean.
not here.
not any more.
lives ago perhaps
she would have been
your second cousin
a lover who murdered you
a woman who passed you on market-day
threw bones to the ground
or stepped over you
as though you were dust or air
some spirit she knew of
but did not counsel.

the first time you see her
a story begins
that has nothing to do with you:
a woman uncle feather knew
and never told you of.
you were so young
and one day he lost the connection
between your question
and her name.

her name could have been anything
but you never would know.
she would pass
and look into your eyes
directly
as if you were not there
as if she knew it
and would not tell.

tak-o-mè-la
tak-o-mè-la

something you hear when she passes
sounds from another living
but there she is
wastreling about you.

someone calls to you.
you watch your thin-woman move
between baskets of fish
and date-wine bottles.

you turn to answer

heart like a brick
down between your knees.

Glossary and Notes

African languages referenced in the poem "History":

Bambara primary language of Mali, spoken by about 7 million people;

Boulou also called *Bulu;* language of the Bulu people of Cameroun. Spoken by about 1 million people in about a half dozen dialects;

Éwondo language of the Éwondo people of Cameroun; about 600,000 speakers and more than a dozen dialects;

Hausa Chadic language spoken in Niger and northern Nigeria; also used as a lingua franca throughout West Africa; about 40 million speakers;

Ki-Kongo language of Angola, Democratic Republic of Congo, Congo Republic and throughout Central Africa; Bantu language with about 7 million speakers;

Kinyarwanda principal language of Rwanda; also spoken in Democratic Republic of Congo, parts of Uganda; Bantu language with 7 million speakers;

Mandara Chadic language spoken in the Mandara Mountains of Cameroun;

Peul also called Fulani; West Atlantic language spoken throughout much of West Africa, primarily Senegal, Gambia, Mauritania, Guinea-Bissau, Burkina Faso, Benin, Mali, Niger, Nigeria, Chad, Cameroun; about 16 million speakers;

Sara group of languages spoken in southern Chad; about 300,000 speakers;

Sérère language spoken primarily in the Siné-Saloum region of Senegal and in Gambia;

Shango also called Sangu; Bantu primary language of Central African Republic;

Toupouri Congo language with about 150,000 speakers;

Tshihiba Congo language of the Tshikapa and Bukwanga regions;

Twi Ashanti language of Ghana;

Wolof primary language of Senegal, also spoken in Gambia and Mauritania; 8–10 million speakers;

Yoruba West African language with more than 20 million speakers in Nigeria, Benin, Togo, Sierra Leone; spoken in the Americas in Brazil, Cuba, Colombia, parts of Puerto Rico.

Affonso, King Affonso V 1432–81, King of Portugal 1438–77.

aguardiente [Spanish/Portuguese *agua* + *ardiente* burning water] cane liquor; coarse, rumlike alcoholic beverage distilled from sugarcane, manufactured and drunk by the slaves of Louisiana, the Caribbean, Latin America; used also as libation or ceremonial or spiritual offering.

altar-room/chapel-room room in or attached to the homes of the **Mothers**, used for religious and spiritual consultation, treatment, healing, meditation, prayer, etc.

avocat [French] lawyer, attorney.

back-parish New Orleans expression designating the speech, mannerisms and behavior of those from the surrounding rural parishes; *perjorative.*

Bahalia (women) [pronounced bah-*HAIL*-ya] now defunct female religious community of New Orleans.

bamboula New Orleans ring dance of Kongo origin, danced by enslaved and free Blacks from the 18th through early 20th centuries, and revived as performance in the late 20th century.

Banganga des Mystères [< Ki-Kongo pl of *nganga* ritual expert + Creole *mystère* spirit, deity] loosely, priests, priestesses, diviners. Banganga heal with roots, herbs, talismans and venerate the most ancient and highest-ranking among the Dead.

banqette [Creole < French, also *banqette, bankette*] paved or boarded sidewalk.

bayou [Louisiana Choctaw, *bayuk*] any of the marshy inlets or outlets of the lakes and other bodies of water throughout Louisiana.

Bayou Goula [Choctaw *bayuk + goula* people] small central Louisiana township near Donaldsonville, less than 3 square miles in area, with a population of about 500.

Bayou la Fou(r)che [< French, *la fourche,* literally, *fork*] Southeast Louisiana outlet, more than 100 miles in length, to the Gulf of Mexico; once known as River Chittimacha.

Bayou Road street running parallel to and following the curve of Bayou St. John; formerly known as the *High or Bayou Road.* See **Congo, Luís,** below.

Bayou St. John ancient site of village of Tchoumatchouma and thus long called Old Indian Portage; once navigable channel connecting the Mississippi River to Lake Pontchartrain located in downtown New Orleans; site of the first fort at what would become New Orleans; traditional slave escape route, and later site of Afro-Orleanian cultural observance and festivals.

Benin, Kingdom of 1156 Kingdom of Benin formally declares that it will "no longer export men, as to continue doing so would strip the kingdom of its power."

Bon Dié [Creole < French *Bon Dieu,* literally, *Good God;* pronounced *boh(n)-djeh*] Great God of the enslaved of New Orleans. Not necessarily identical to the Christian God, Bon Dié is all-powerful, all-knowing.

breaking of the season annual, often torrential rains immediately preceding spring and autumn, traditionally recognized as the beginning of the new season and often accompanied by high winds and street flooding. These rains and the seasons they announce symbolize birth, death, transformation and more.

Brown, Sterling 1901–89, African American poet and champion of African American vernacular language, music, crafts and culture; longtime Howard University professor of literature; best known for *Southern Road* (Harcourt, Brace 1932), the critical study *Negro Poetry and Drama; and the Negro in American Fiction* (Atheneum, 1972) and *The Collected Poems of Sterling A. Brown* (Northwestern, 1996).

Butcher-Spanish now-defunct, creolized Spanish of New Orleans, introduced via Cuba during the Spanish colonial era, broadly, 1763–1803.

cane liquor heavy, rum-like alcoholic beverage distilled from sugar cane manufactured and drunk by the enslaved throughout Louisiana and much of the Caribbean and Latin America; frequently used also as ritual offering or libation. See **aguardiente**, above.

canne à sucre [Creole < French, sugarcane, pronounced *kahn-ah-souk*] sugar cane; Creole endearment, especially poignant because of the intensity of labor in Louisiana sugarcane country.

Cape of Good Hope the southwesternmost point of Africa first rounded by Barolomeo Diaz in 1488 and called by him *Cabo de Tormentas* or "Cape of Storms"; later renamed *Cabo de Boa Esperança* by João II of Portugal, in hope of establishing a direct route from there to India and the Spice Islands.

Cão, Diogo ca 1450–86 Portuguese navigator; first European known to have explored the western coast of Africa and the Congo River, 1482–83 and 1484–86.

castles holding forts or slave castles referenced in the poem "History":

Cape Coast Ghana; erected 1653 for the Swedish Africa Company;

Cabo de Delgado Mozambique; the trade continued there until 1877;

Elmina Ghana; erected 1482 by the Portuguese;

Fort Osu Ghana; erected 1661 at Accra by the Danes;

Île de Gorée/Goree Island home of Senegal's famed *Maison des Esclaves* ("Slave House"). The first *Slave House* was erected in 1536 by the Portuguese. Following French conquest in the 1670s, the newer *Maison des Esclaves* was erected between 1780 and 1784;

São Tomé erected 1575 São Tomé e Principe (island nation in the Gulf of Guinea) by the Portuguese; now the São Tomé National Museum;

São Vicente one of the Windward Islands of Cape Verde. Originally settled by the Portuguese in 1456, Cape Verde played a major role in the Atlantic Slave Trade because of its location midway between the western coast of Africa and Europe and the Americas.

catalpa tree large, deciduous, soft-wood tree bearing broad, heart-shaped leaves, long pods, showy yellow or white flowers, and capable of growing in sun or shade as well as a variety of climates and soil conditions.

chamy-bag [Creole < French *chamois* (fabric)] small or large pouch, usually with drawstring, containing one's personal medicine, made up of various natural and sacred objects and substances, and originally made of chamois fabric.

chapel-room See **altar-room**, above.

Charity (Hospital) founded 1726 in New Orleans, originally as l'Hôpital des Pauvres de la Charité, it was administered by the Sisters of Charity from 1832; served the poor of the City for more than 250 years; known locally simply as "Charity"; famed and later infamous for its treatment of mental illness.

City, the New Orleans; common usage among those born and reared in New Orleans, for whom rural Louisiana often is unknown or mistrusted as a kind of backwater or wilderness.

Code Noir, le the *Black Code* applied throughout the French slave colonies beginning 1687, in New Orleans 1724. Among stipulations concerning the enslaved are: mandatory Catholic religious instruction; the right to marry; suspension of labor on Sundays; striking and causing a visible bruise to a master, mistress or their children punishable by death.

Colbert, Jean Baptiste 1619–83 author of *le Code Noir;* key figure in the history of European mercantilism; minister of finance for twenty-two years under King Louis XIV; credited with restoring the French economy by increasing trade, including the French slave trade.

Colón, Cristóval or *Cristóbal* 1451–1506 Italian (*Cristoforo Colombo*) mariner supported in his explorations by the Spanish monarchy (see **Isabel**); credited with discovery of the Americas (1492) and opening the way for the Atlantic Slave Trade.

companies, slave trading referenced in "History":

> **American Islands** *Compagnie des Îles d'Amérique,* ca 1635–50; Cardinal Richelieu among founder/stockholders;

French Senegal *Compagnie de Sénégal,* 1672 (original Company 1626), France; held monopoly on trade from Senegal River to Sierra Leone; more than 20 slaving vessels employed by 1679;

Guiana 1619 by Robert, Earl of Warwick, England;

New Cayenne 1777 (original Cayenne Company 1651), France at (French) Guiana;

New France 1602 France at Montréal, Canada;

Royal African *Company of Royal Adventurers Trading to Africa,* chartered 1660, England; created by the Stuart monarchy; James, Duke of York (brother to Charles II) and London merchants guilds. Although the Royal African Company lost its charter in 1698, it continued in the slave trade until 1731, having transported some 100,000+ African captives and having been responsible for the naming of the English gold coin, the *guinea.*

Santo Domingo 1698 France;

Second Louisiana 1712, France.

Congo, Luís (*Louis, Jean-Louis*) free Kongo-man, employed in 1726 in New Orleans as Keeper of the High or Bayou Road, where he established an estate; the official executioner of slaves escaping New Orleans via Bayou St. John; said to have died mysteriously at the hands of slaves.

Congo, Tiamca, Matinga, Colango, Bambara, Nago, Senegal, Creole, Negro designations of Africans transported as slaves to Louisiana during the Spanish Colonial period.

conju [Creole < French *conjure*] the practice of conjuring; calling forth or calling on spirits.

Cooke, Sam 1931–64 African American soul and gospel singer (with the Soul Stirrers) generally cited as the first Soul music superstar and often credited as the Father of Soul Music. His 1960 composition "Chain Gang" was one of many original hits. The version quoted here is from the album, *Sam Cooke Live at the Harlem Square Club 1963* (New York: RCA Victor, 1985).

cross in the road the crossroads; the place where one road or pathway intersects another; metaphor for spiritual challenge, transformation, transcendence.

Damballah [Fon, *Dan* or *Dan Bada;* also Kongo, *Da* or *Dan;* also Kongo, *Ndamba,* literally, *rainbow serpent*] deity who mediates between the worlds of the living and dead.

day's work woman in New Orleans, a maid, laundress or other woman servant hired and paid a small wage for a single day or half-day. During the 18th and 19th centuries, poorer free Black women hired themselves out in this manner to wealthier households and could generally be found at any of the open or public marketplaces of the City. This practice continued well into the early 20th century.

Dent, Thomas Covington 1932–98 African American poet, playwright, author and activist; best known for poems "For Lil Louis" and "Return to English Turn" (*Magnolia Street,* 1976); the drama *Ritual Murder* (1968); and the study, *Southern Journey: a Return to the Civil Rights Movement* (William Morrow, 1997).

Devil is beating his wife again, the ["She burned the beans and the rice again."] lyrics based on the subtropical phenomenon of rain occurring while the sun is brightly shining. New Orleans lore has it that this phenomenon occurs when the Devil beats his wife for having burned his lunch of red beans and rice.

DOM-TOM [French acronym for *les Départements d'Outre-mer et les Territoires d'Outre-mer*] French Overseas Departments and Territories include the longtime colonial possessions of Guadeloupe, Martinique, Guyane, St. Pierre et Miquelon, Mayotte, Réunion, Nouvelle-Calédonie, Wallis and Futuna, and French Polynesia.

Dona Felipa (Perestrello e Moniz, Lady) Portuguese noblewoman and wife of Columbus. Historians generally report that she died shortly after the birth of their son Diego, the only legitimate child of Columbus, in 1480 or 1481.

douceur, ma [French, *my sweetness*] Creole endearment.

encomienda [Spanish, *commission, protectorate*] beginning in 1493, system by which conquistadores established Spanish rule and assumed authority over Native peoples of the Americas, including forced labor, imposition of taxation and Catholic religion.

Érzulie Haitian representation of Yoruba deity Ochun or Oshun, goddess of river waters.

faubourg [French *false town, false borough, suburb*] any of the early, named suburbs and residential districts of New Orleans, such as **Faubourg Tremé** or Faubourg Marigny.

Faubourg Tremé first suburb of the original city of New Orleans (*Vieux Carré*), settled in the 1710s by free Blacks, now part of downtown New Orleans.

fix [New Orleans traditional religion] to *fix* or *put a fix on* (a person or situation); to bring under one's personal power and control.

Fra Bartolomeo (de las Casas) 1484–1566 Dominican friar praised for his defense of Native peoples of the Americas in such works as *Brevísima relación de la destrucción de las Indias* (*Short Account of the Destruction of the Indies*, 1552), *Apologética historia summaria de las gentes destas Indias* (*Apologetic Summary History of the People of these Indies*, 1566, although originally a section of the earlier work) and others. Arguing that Native peoples of the Americas should not be enslaved because they possessed nobility, higher intelligence and divine souls, he strongly urged King Carlos V of Spain that African peoples, whom he asserted possessed no such human characteristics, be enslaved instead.

Fray Bartolome de Albornoz (dissents) 1520–1612 University of Mexico founding professor of law, "Father of Mexican Jurisconsult," and Dominican priest; among the first of a small number of clerics to argue against the capture, sale and enslavement of Africans. In the chapter, "De la Esclavitud," in *Arte de los Contratos* (1573, Valencia), de Albornoz condemns the slave trade and attacks the opinion popular among 15th and 16th century religions that the trade was necessary to save heathen souls, arguing that only Africans were capable of determining their cultural and religious state; that the Church had an obligation neither to condone nor to ignore the trade, but to support liberation from oppression; and that law is based in the presumption of natural liberty. *Arte de los Contratos* was placed on the *Index Librorum Prohibitorum*, the list of books officially banned by the Inquisition.

gallery [pronounced *ga(l)'ry*] Louisiana designation for the circular and semi-circular porches common to large houses and accessible from within the house and surrounding yard or gardens. Commonly, there are *full, half* and *¾ galleries*.

Guanahani original name of Native Americans referred to as "Caribs" and for whom the Caribbean Sea is named; traditionally portrayed as excessively warlike as well as cannibalistic. Guantanamexe and Guanaguahana are royal names assigned the elder and younger daughters of the fictional prince of the Caribs, here known only as the "last of the **Guanahani**."

hands on, to put one's [Creole] to caress, make love to, enthrall.

Hayden, Robert 1913–80 African American poet, perhaps best known for the epic

"Middle Passage," "Runagate Runagate" and the sonnet "Frederick Douglass." See his *Collected Poems,* edited by Frederick Glaysher (Liveright, 1985).

hidden lily a tropical plant of the ginger (*Zingiberaceae*) family having yellow, pink, white or purple cone-shaped flowers.

Isabel Queen Isabel I; Isabela la Católica de España 1451–1504 queen of Spain 1474–1504; originator (with Ferdinand) of the Inquisition; patroness of **Columbus** (see **Colón**).

Jackson Louisiana State Insane Asylum, founded 1847; later Louisiana Hospital for the Insane at Jackson, Louisiana; known for housing and treatment of so-called criminally insane.

levee any of the grassy, boarded, paved or walled embankments along the network of canals designed to prevent flooding should the Mississippi River rise; also traditional sites of festivals and recreational gatherings.

lifting up in New Orleans funerary tradition, the practice of holding up images or other tokens and symbolizing worldly release of the spirit of the deceased.

loa [Yoruba] spirit, deity.

Loa-mamma, loa-water-mamma feminine deity of New Orleans, invoked against rain and flood, as in the traditional chant, *"Shallow water, loa-mamma!"*

Louis Louis XVI 1754–93 king of France 1774–92 during the French Revolution of 1789–91; executed by guillotine January 1793; execution of his spouse, Marie Antoinette, followed in October of that year.

Lyrics cited:

"The Fabric of Our Lives": from the Cotton, Incorporated television advertising jingle:*"The touch / the feel of cotton / the fabric of our lives."*

"Fodder on My Wings": *Fodder on My Wings,* Carrere (France), 1982; music and lyrics by Nina Simone.

"I left my hat / in Haiti!": "I Left My Hat in Haiti" (music by Burton Lane, lyrics by Alan Lerner) song and dance routine by Fred Astaire with Jane Powell and chorus, in the movie-musical *Royal Wedding.* MGM, 1951.

"if you live right": "If You Live Right (Heaven Belongs to You)" (traditional) as "If You Pray Right," Nina Simone. *Let It Be Me.* PolyGram Records, 1987.

"ages ago / last night / when we were young!": "Last Night When We Were Young" (music by Harold Arlen, lyrics by Edgar Yipsel Harburg) Sarah Vaughan. *The Essential Sarah Vaughan: The Great Songs.* Verve Records, 1959.

"Someday We'll All Be Free," (music by Donny Hathaway, lyrics by Edward Howard) Donny Hathaway. *Extension of a Man.* Atco, 1973.

"outside-a you / there is no / place to go": "Be My Husband" (music and lyrics by Andy Stroud) Nina Simone. *Let It Be Me.* PolyGram Records, 1987.

Manchac [Choctaw *back way in*] a large and once desolated swamp situated west of Lake Pontchartrain, reported to have served as haven to maroons and other fugitives; known also as Swamp Manchac and Manchac Swamp.

Manchac Pass once unpaved dirt and shell road originating west of Lake Pontchartrain and leading north to the Louisana/Mississippi state line, eventually paved over and appearing on maps as Highway 51; now a seldom use scenic route; known also as *Pass Manchac.*

Mardi Gras Indian Afro-Orleanian secret societies dating from ca 1880 and employing ritual music, dance, language and attire, clearly defined hierarchy of leadership and succession, embracing Black political resistance.

ma-ròn [Creole *maroon, brown*] the dark chestnut or reddish-brown skin color said to have been typical of **maroons**; the color brown. See **maroon**, below.

maroon [< Spanish *cimarron* wild horse] escaped slave or community of escaped slaves living in seclusion in the swamplands, wilderness or forests. In New Orleans, maroons and their descendants were believed to possess special knowledge of and spiritual power from African ancestors and, therefore, regarded with awe or fear.

Mbanza Kongo [Ki-Kongo] in Kongo cosmology, the ideal capital to which the holy departed return, situated on a hilltop and ruled by a mighty and beloved king; also, the ancient capital of the Kongo kingdom re-named São Salvador under Portuguese colonial rule in the mid-16th century.

M'dear [Creole *mamman* + English *dear* mother dear] mamma, mamman; endearment also frequently conferred on older women.

Mesachabe [Algonquin, *Father of Waters*] Mississippi River.

mòn, pòn [Creole < French *mamman, papa*] mother, father; familiar or contemptuous usage, depending on the context.

Monk, Thelonious Sphere 1917–82 jazz composer, pianist, arranger, bandleader and founder of modern jazz and Bebop. *Solo Monk* (Columbia Record, 1965) and *Standards* (Columbia Records, released posthumously in 1989) are two of his best known, most beloved recordings.

monkey-grass low, flowering tropical grass used to edge gardens and prevent weed growth.

Montesquieu Charles-Louis de Secondat, Baron de Montesquieu 1689–1755 French author and philosopher; major proponent of Liberalism; best known for 1748 publication of *De l'Esprit des Lois* ("Of the Spirit of the Law"), placed on the Roman Catholic Church's Index of Forbidden Books in 1751. Immensely popular, the work went through twenty editions during his lifetime. The quoted lines—examples of popular excuses for the need for African slavery—are from the chapter entitled "le Droit de Rendre les Nègres Esclaves" ("The Right to Make Slaves of the Blacks").

Mother [New Orleans traditional religion] a hereditary spiritual healer.

mourning dove [zoological, *Zenaida macroura*] light grey or brown dove, so called because of its distinctively eerie cooing. In New Orleans lore, mourning doves nesting above doorways indicate imminent death in the family.

Mpemba [Ki-Kongo *chalk, white substance* (the color white representing death, the dead, mourning)] Kongo Land of the Dead, represented as a vast body of water. In Kongo cosmology, the earth is a mountain situated above **Mpemba**.

Mystère [Creole *(the) Mystery*] Great God Almighty.

nation any Black person of national origin outside of the US. A man or woman from Haiti or Senegal, for instance, is not called a "foreigner," but "a nation."

Nature [New Orleans traditional religion] sexual energy of an individual, said to be capable of endowing characteristics of greatness or madness, depending on how it is channeled.

Navidad, la [Spanish *Christmas*] name given by **Columbus** to the first settlement on Santo Domingo [Haiti] because, he said, it was "born" Christmas 1492.

Ngola [< Kimbundu *ruler*] Angola; former name of 14th to 17th century capital city of Ndongo.

Nicky Vth, Pope 4 January 1444 Pope Nicholas V grants king of Portugal the right to open trade between Kongo and Portugal. Later that year, African captives are taken from Mauritania to Portugal.

Olurun See **Bon Dié**, above.

panniér large basket made of straw, wood or cane and equipped with handles and a lid, used for transporting food and small market goods.

Papa Legba [Creole < Yoruba *Elegba, Elegbara, Elegua*] representation of Yoruba deity *Elegba* or *Elegua*, guardian of the crossroads, the sacred doorway, and emissary of the gods; justice personified.

paquet d'medecin [Creole *medicine bag*] small or large pouch or sack containing one's personal medicine. See **chamy bag**, above.

Passages quoted in the poem "History":

> "that MAN has indeed become the coin of Africa": "I have no hesitation in say-ing, that three fourths of the slaves sent abroad from Africa are the fruit of na-tive wars, fomented by the avarice and temptation of our own race. I cannot exculpate any commercial nation from this sweeping censure. We stimulate the negro's passions by the introduction of wants and fancies never dreamed of by the simple native, while slavery was an institution of domestic need and comfort alone. But what was once a luxury has now ripened into an absolute necessity; so that MAN, in truth, has become the coin of Africa, and the 'legal tender' of a brutal trade."
> —"The African Slave Trade," *DeBow's Review: Agricultural, com-mercial, industrial progress and resources,* March 1855 [vol. 18, no. 3, pp. 297–305].

> In 1846, James D. B. DeBow, a native of Charleston, South Carolina, began publishing his pro- slavery magazine in New Orleans. Originally titled the *Commercial Review of the South and West,* the journal eventually came to be known as *DeBow's Review.* From 1853 to 1857, it was published in Washing-ton, D.C., due to DeBow's appointment there as director of the U.S. Census Bureau. At the start of the Civil War, *DeBow's Review* was the most widely circulated southern periodical.

"You ain't seen nothing yet": In 1922, Al Jolson (1886-1950) recorded the Bud DeSylva composition "You Ain't Heard Nothing Yet." The line, "You ain't *heard* nothing yet" [emphasis mine], spoken by Jolson, became the first words spoken in a feature film (*The Jazz Singer*, Warner Brothers, 1927), propelled him to instant stardom and became his entr'acte lead-in. Comedic admirers and imitators of Jolson have frequently misquoted the line as "You ain't *seen* nothing yet!" He is best remembered, however, for his Vaudeville blackface persona. Entertainment legend has it that he adopted blackface because he believed audiences laughed more for African American performers than for whites. Jolson is still considered by many to have been the best Vaudeville performer of all time.

Pointe-à-la-Hâche [< French *pointe* tip + *à la* + *hache* axe, letter *h*] axe-blade, referring to the axe or h-shape of the area where land meets water; village in Plaquemines **Parish**, Louisiana; population fewer than 300.

prayer-band term applied to any "renegade" Christian religious group organized by women.

rains See **breaking of the season**, above.

Rampart (Street) broad street running north-south and separating the Vieux Carré (now *French Quarter*) from **Faubourg Tremé**.

read, to or **to be read** to give or receive spiritual interpretation of one's life, present and future difficulties, health matters, etc., by a **Mother** or spiritual healer; consequently, to be advised on how to counteract undesirable developments in one's affairs thorugh performance of prescribed rituals.

Répétez s'il-vous-plaît [French "Please repeat (after me)"] expression used in teaching by rote. See **tous à la fois**, below.

requerimiento [Spanish, *demand, injunction*] statement of Spanish sovereignty over the Americas, claiming Divine Right under rule of the Catholic Church, as pronounced in the May 1493 papal bull of Pope Alexander VI.

River Nzadi [*zaire* < Ki-Kongo *nzadi, nzere River to Swallow All Rivers*] Congo River; second longest river of the African continent, flowing approximately 3000 miles through Zambia, Democratic Republic of Congo (formerly known as *Zaire*) and Republic of Congo, and emptying into the Atlantic Ocean.

River Road site of the earliest indigo and later sugar plantations and refineries of Louisiana, and a regular site of slave rebellion, running approximately 75 miles along both sides of the Mississippi River from Baton Rouge into and through New Orleans.

St. Expedite/Expeditus [pronounced *ex-pe-deet*] grantor of speedy response; a "false" saint of the Catholic Church. According to Catholic lore, a statue of a foot soldier intended for a crucifixion scene arrived separately from other figures, marked with the word "Expedite," mistaken for his name.

San Malo, Juan d. 1784, rebel leader of a maroon colony at Chef Menteur, on the eastern outskirts of New Orleans. When captured, San Malo and his followers were hanged. A major figure in New Orleans and regional history, he is memorialized as a martyr in such ballads as "Aye! Zheun Gens!" In "The Business of Pursuit," I have created a relationship between San Malo and **Luís Congo**.

Saint James (Parish) See **Parishes**, above.

Schoelcher, Victor 1804–93 author of French *Decree of Abolition,* 1848, and Caribbean assimilation policy; touted as "savior" of francophone Caribbean and defender of civil rights, the "inheritance of 1789."

Seven Sisters a family of holy women said to have lived in and around New Orleans at the turn of the 20th century.

shallow water loa-mamma See **loa**, above.

side-alley [downtown New Orleans usage] paved or unpaved passageway on one or both sides of a house and separating it, with or without a wall, fence or hedge, from neighboring houses and yards, and providing access to a side or rear enteance to the house.

sidelight one of the two narraow doors on either side of the main door to a house. A common architectural feature of New Orleans houses, **sidelights** are left open during the long warm weather months, both for added ventilation and easy access to the outdoors; typically used also to observe activities of neighbors and passersby.

Simone, Nina 1933–2003 classical pianist, jazz and Freedom Movement composer, singer and Civil Rights Movement activist. The line "heaven did not come to me either" is a variation on a lyric from her rendition of the traditional hymn, "If You Pray Right (Heaven Belongs to You)." The lines "outside-a you / there is no / place to go" are from Andy Stroud's "Be My Husband," as sung by Simone.

slave-brick, slave-bricked descriptive of any road, street, building or other structure constructed all or in part of the common red brick found throughout New Orleans and originally manufactured by the slaves of the city's first brick factory located in **Faubourg Tremé.** The handiwork of slave ancestors, the bricks are said to possess spiritual power, and is used most frequently to bless and purify the homes of the faithful by rubbing across steps and doorways; used also for drawing and marking.

slave castles See **castles**, above.

Spanish Fort site of Spanish colonial fort on **Bayou St. John** at the northwest outlet to Lake Pontchartrain; now part of City Park in the area bounded by Robert E. Lee, Ibis and Beauregard Streets.

Square, Jackson formerly the French colonial *Place d'Armes* and Spanish colonial *Plaza de Armas,* seat of New Orleans colonial government, during the 18th and 19th centuries; situated opposite the Cabildo, and the primary site of public torture and execution of the enslaved; renamed in honor of Andrew Jackson following the Battle of New Orleans, 1815.

Sterling See **Brown, Sterling**, above.

tignon [Creole pronounced *teen-yo(h)n*] elaborate headdresses, styled with sequins, jewels, feathers, etc., worn by 18th and 19th century New Orleans free Black women.

Times-Picayune [English *times* + Provençal *picaioun* small coin, cheap, petty, mean] one-time daily New Orleans newspaper.

tous à la fois [French *"All together (now)!"*] phrase traditionally used for teaching by rote. See **Répétez s'il-vous-plaît**, above.

trahison des clercs, la [French "the betrayal of the clerks"] expression traditionally used to refer to the tendency of the mulatto class of the francophone Caribbean to side with the whites.

van-van [Creole < French *vervain,* pronounced *vah(n)-vah(n)*] medicinal herb, said to promote affection and fond memory.

Vaughan, Sarah Lois 1924–90 jazz vocalist; winner of Grammy and Jazz Masters Awards; nicknamed "The Divine (One)" for her four-octave range, singular brand of scat-singing, warm vibrato, purity of tone and unparalleled mastery of long-breath singing.

vèvè the sign, symbol or signature of a deity in the form of a diagram, series of ideographs or other visual representation.

yellow-cotton light-weight and inexpensive but durable unbleached cotton or muslin fabric used to make women's and girls' shifts, simple house-dresses and summer nightgowns, as well as napkins, dishcloths, hand towels, etc.

Author Biography

Brenda Marie Osbey is a poet and essayist working in English and French, and the author of five previous collections. She is the recipient of the American Book Award for *All Saints: New and Selected Poems* in 1998 and the Langston Hughes Award in 2014.

She has received fellowships and awards from the National Endowment for the Arts, the Louisiana Division of the Arts, the New Orleans Jazz and Heritage Foundation and others, and has been a resident fellow of the MacDowell Colony, the Millay Colony, Virginia Center for the Creative Arts, Fine Arts Work Center in Provincetown, the Bunting Institute of Radcliffe College, Harvard University, the Camargo Foundation at Cassis and Maison Dora Maar at Ménerbes, France.

From 2005–2007, she served as the first peer-selected poet laureate of Louisiana. Osbey is currently Distinguished Visiting Professor of Africana Studies at Brown University.

CPSIA information can be obtained
at www.ICGtesting.com
Printed in the USA
FFOW02n2116270116
20869FF